Caspar Schwenckfeld's *Passional*

A Translation for Contemporary Readers

Anabaptist Devotional Texts in Translation

—accessible renditions of historical texts
for contemporary readers—

Volume 1. *Caspar Schwenckfeld's Passional: A Translation for Contemporary Readers.* Edited and translated by H. H. Drake Williams III. Pandora Press, 2025.

Caspar Schwenckfeld's *Passional*

A Translation for Contemporary Readers

Edited and translated by
H. H. Drake Williams III

PANDORA
PRESS

CASPAR SCHWENCKFELD'S PASSIONAL
A TRANSLATION FOR CONTEMPORARY READERS
EDITED AND TRANSLATED BY H. H. DRAKE WILLIAMS III

ISBN-13: 978-1-77873-031-3

Editing, interior, and cover design by Maxwell Kennel

Copyright © 2025 Pandora Press
Published by Pandora Press
All rights reserved.
www.pandorapress.com

Table of Contents

Acknowledgments _____ 7

Introduction _____ 9

   Caspar Schwenckfeld _____ 10

   Schwenckfeld's Passional in Historical Context ____ 12

   Current Translation _____ 19

   Suggestions for Use _____ 23

Foreword _____ 25

Prayers in Christ's Suffering and Passion _____ 27

Appendices _____ 103

   The Scripture Texts Employed for Meditation in Schwenckfeld's Passional _____ 104

   The Presentation of Jesus Christ _____ 107

   Correspondence with the Lord's Prayer _____ 112

   Schwenckfeld on Prayer, Confession, and Thanksgiving _____ 115

   Addressing Antisemitic Elements _____ 123

The Apostles' Creed, Nicene Creed, and the Chalcedonian Statement _____ 130

Editor's Reflection _____ 134

Bibliography _____ 137

Acknowledgments

No publication emerges without the assistance of others. Several are worthy of special mention. As the reader will see, this *Passional* was written during Schwenckfeld's exile. The fact that he wrote it and circulated while avoiding those who were after him is important. Those who have made it possible for contemporary readers to read the document had preserved it in the *Corpus Schwenckfeldianorum*. Elmer Ellsworth Schultz Johnson was the editor of the specific volume in which the *Passional* is found.

The first translation of Schwenckfeld's *Passional* book was done by John Joseph Stoudt, and it was published in 1961, on the 400th anniversary of Caspar Schwenckfeld's death. Several people kept Schwenckfeld's *Passional* accessible for modern readers: Rev. Dr. Jack Rothenberger referred to it in his ministry at Central Schwenkfelder Church, and Dr. Peter Erb promoted the value of this book through his work with the Schwenkfelder Library and Heritage Center.

In recent times, several Schwenkfelders have taken interest in prayer as it is expressed by Caspar Schwenckfeld. They include George Meschter, Peter Colvin, Jerry Heebner, Bill Sabota, Ruth Balthozer, Joanne Jalowy, and my father H. H. Drake Williams, Jr. My wife, Andrea Williams helped with the proofreading. The Schwenkfelder Ministerium, Rev. Nick Pence, Rev. Alfred Duncan, Rev. Leslie Mamas, Rev. Julian Scavetti, and Rev. Dr. David McKinley contributed invaluable feedback. Dr. Allen Viehmeyer, who is the Associate Director of Research at the Schwenkfelder Library and Heritage Center, read this manuscript several times and made helpful comments.

This book is dedicated to Rev. Dr. David McKinley. He has been a faithful leader of a weekly prayer meeting for many years at Central Schwenkfelder Church in Lansdale, PA.

May we all be consistent in prayer.

Introduction

Schwenkfelder tradition contains many written documents that could be valuable for Christian experience and faithfulness in our time. Radical Reformation literature reflects a deep interest in the meaning of the text of the Bible but also the importance of both understanding Scripture in the heart and then expressing it in everyday life. Furthermore, the intense emotional experience reflected in these writings can resonate in a culture where many people are seeking deeper spiritual experiences.

Unfortunately, much of Schwenkfelder literature has been less accessible to the broader Christian public. Some of Schwenckfeld's writing remains in German fraktur font in the *Corpus Schwenkfeldianorum* or in seventeenth or eighteenth-century German script. At times, when a translation has been provided, it is often difficult for readers to understand its complex sentence structures and archaic wording.

The goal of this booklet is to take a translation of one of Caspar Schwenckfeld's devotional writings and make it more accessible to a general audience for practical and devotional use. In that interest, the introduction below will help to frame the *Passional.*

Caspar Schwenckfeld

Caspar Schwenckfeld (1489–1561) was a lesser-known Protestant Reformer in Silesia, Germany. He was not a theologian, but rather a nobleman. In 1518, he experienced a spiritual awakening. From that point onward, he became an avid student of Scripture and a follower of Martin Luther.

Schwenckfeld and Luther agreed about many things regarding the Catholic Church at the time. They did not affirm a pope and they reacted negatively to the selling of indulgences. Both Schwenckfeld and Luther also called Christians to a purer understanding of the faith. Despite their similarities, Luther and Schwenckfeld disagreed with each other due to their perspective on the Eucharist, and thus, separated from each other. Due to the conflict with

Luther and then his followers, Schwenckfeld went into voluntary exile, which lasted thirty-two years.

Although he was in exile, Schwenckfeld continued to write about the proper understanding of the Christian faith, which he called "the Middle Way." This approach attempted to create a middle course between the Catholics and the followers of Martin Luther. His main concern was that the teachings of these groups were diverting attention away from the person of Jesus Christ. Moreover, he thought that their teachings were pointing to external religious symbols rather than to the need for the heart to change.

Besides his great interest in the person of Jesus Christ, Caspar Schwenckfeld had other emphases in his Christian thinking. He believed in the practical nature of the Christian faith. In other words, he thought that Christian doctrine, while important, must be expressed in faith and love. Furthermore, he suggested that a sincere faith must lead Christians to imitate Christ. He was a great advocate of personal prayer and Bible study. When he wrote about Christian practice, he expressed his viewpoints with many references to both the Old and New Testaments and in relation to the Apostles' Creed and the Lord's Prayer.

Although many of his interests may resonate with many contemporary Christians, Schwenckfeld fell out of favor with other Reformers at the time. He was anathematized at the Schmackald League and became a religious fugitive. His followers separated from other church connections and then formed small societies. Eventually, they fled Silesia to Herrnhut in Saxony, Germany. Then they passed through the Netherlands, England, and eventually settled in southeastern Pennsylvania, USA.

Schwenckfeld's Passional *in Historical Context*

Caspar Schwenckfeld produced documents that ministered to the common person and not just to academics or clergy. One of these is his *Deutsch Passional unsern Herren Jeus Christi. Mit schönen tröstlichen Gebetlein und Figuren.* In English, this is the *German Passion of our Lord Jesus Christ with beautiful, comforting prayers and illustrations.* His *Passional* was written in 1539.

At this point in the timeline of his life, he had already fallen out with Martin Luther. He was also in self-imposed exile for ten years.[1] While in the city of Ulm (1534–1539), he was under criticism by those in the city and elsewhere. A commission was formed to consider whether it was still possible for Schwenckfeld to remain within the city. His publishing and writing were further curtailed. Schwenckfeld left the city of Ulm late in September 1539, and moved around to various places, visiting friends in southern Germany. The sense of suffering that he was experiencing at the time is likely reflected in the *Passional.*

Meditation upon the passion of Jesus Christ was always an important part of his ministry to others. In a letter to a friend who was on the brink of losing his faith, he encouraged the man to draw close to Christ and his word, which he said cannot fail. To help his friend's lack of spiritual strength, he writes this in 1523.

> . . . you should frequently read the New Testament and particularly the parts that set forth his Passion. Yes, every day you should

---

[1] S. G. Schultz, *Caspar Schwenckfeld von Ossig*, 239–52.

> utter your prayer and meditate upon it, not perfunctorily, but with the deepest aspiration of your heart, so that you may be fully reminded of the sufferings of Christ and of his Word. By this medium then, you will form with you and unfading and abiding picture of the satisfaction he has wrought by his bitter death. Indeed, you must regard your sins as laid upon his cross; then the blessed conviction, that it is well with you, will come into your consciousness; for the Lord Christ is kind and merciful.[2]

His interest in meditation on the passion of Christ agreed with others who focused on this event in Jesus's life. Saint Augustine (AD 355–430) found the meditation upon the passion of the Lord provided a great remedy for the sins of his flesh. Saint Bonaventure (AD 1221–1274) believed that meditating upon the passion of Jesus broke down the callous hearts of sinners. Saint Albert the Great (AD 1260–1280) believed that meditating on the

---

[2] C. Schwenckfeld, "Translation of Letter to a friend who is on the point of losing his faith," in *Corpus Schwenckfeldianorum* 1. Edited by C. D. Hartranft (Leipzig/Breitkopf & Härtel: Board of Publication of the Schwenkfelder Church, 1907), 65.

Passion was more valuable than fasting a whole year. Speaking about the passion, Bernard of Clairvaux (AD 1190–1153) believed that he might be less aware of the importance of the event. He did not realize the severity of the heavenly sentence given to him. Thus, he worried that he would make light of it and took time to meditate upon it regularly.

The Reformers continued to focus on the passion of Christ. In 1519, Martin Luther preached on Christ's passion. His messages reflected on key events during the Passion, such as: Jesus's time on the Mount of Olives, Peter's Denial, Jesus's time before Pilate, being nailed to the cross, and his body being taken down from the cross. In his sermons, Luther explains the events that took place in Christ's life and then provides some devotional consequences.[3]

The connection with the time of the Reformation is particularly evident within Luther's sermons on the Passion. He places his explanation over and against the Roman Catholic church of the time, which emphasized the torture of Christ and penance. He

---

[3] See M. Luther, *Sermons on the Passion of Christ: Translated from the German* (Rockland, IL: Lutheran Augustana, 1871).

also repeated that Christians should be thankful for Jesus's suffering. There is no mention of things associated with the medieval Catholic church such as penance, indulgences, or transubstantiation.

Luther's messages on the passion of Jesus Christ provide pastoral commentary on main aspects of the events surrounding Jesus's death. Similarly to Schwenckfeld's *Passional*, Luther emphasizes the importance of conversion. He does not, however, produce individual prayers for each event of the passion like Schwenckfeld's *Passional*.

The general Christian population during the Reformation became interested in the events of the Passion. Passion plays would evolve in the following century, such as the passion play at Oberammergau in 1634 which continues every decade to this day.[4] These plays kept the events of the final week of Jesus's life in a prominent place before the people.

---

[4] See further website about the Passion Play in Oberammergau, Germany: Passionspiele Oberammergau.
https://www.passionsspiele-oberammergau.de/en/home
(Accessed: 20 February 2025).

Besides Luther, many others had written and preached on the passion of Christ.[5] Schwenckfeld's *Passional* reflects his great interest in the passion itself. Schwenckfeld not only told the story of the passion, however. His consideration of the event led him to add prayers of reflection on the event. In his work, he incorporates prayers from Cornelius Crocus, a Dutch theologian who became a Jesuit and who himself wrote prayers about the passion.[6] Sixty of these are represented in Schwenckfeld's *Passional*. Having both the biblical text of the passion and prayers together made Schwenckfeld's *Passional* distinct from Martin Luther's sermons which did not have prayers accompanying the

---

[5] See Bernard, *Passio Domini Jesu Christi secundum quatouor Evangelia* (1502); J. Knoblouch, *Der text des passions. oder lidens Christi, oß den vier evangelisten zusammen inn ein son bracht mit schönen figüren* (Basel: Knoblauch, 1506); U. Pinder, *Speculum passionis domini nostri Jesu Christi, cum textu quattuor euangelistarum et doctorum glossis* (1507). Also consider sermons such as: Gabriel Biel, *Passionis dominice sermo historialis notabilis atque praeclarus* (Germany: Heumann, 1509); Johannis de Gerson, *Sermo de passione dominic: Nuper e Gallico in latium traductus* (Strassburg: Schürer, 1510). See further E. E. Johnson, "Deutsch Passional," in *Corpus Schwenckfeldianorum*, Vol. 6. Board of Publication: Leipzig, Breitkopf & Härtel, 1922), 652–53.

[6] Crocus's prayers were in Alardus, *Piae precationes in passionem Jesu Christi* (Amsterdam, 1532).

biblical text. In his writing, Schwenckfeld also incorporated woodcut illustrations.

Schwenckfeld's *Passional* was an important means for keeping the significance of the death of Christ at the forefront for his followers. Otherwise, he was concerned that the hearts of people would grow cold to its truth, or even worse, that they would forget it. In his *Passional*, he not only recalled the narrative of Christ's death, but he provided his own devotional meditations. He focused on individual Christians' need for belief that Christ suffered on account of our sins, which he bore in obedience to the Father's will and out of love. If Christians understood the depths of this event, he thought, it would move them to feel sorrow in their souls and to feel joy toward God because of how he had reconciled Christians to himself through the death of his Son. Then, for Schwenckfeld, once this relationship was understood, it would lead to faithful living.

Schwenckfeld attempts to lead the reader through a heartfelt experience of Christ's suffering. This culminates when he encourages his reader to seek personal conversion. In the final prayer, he encourages the reader to pray, "Even though I came from the death of sin, please grant to me that I may walk in newness of life."

Current Translation

Schwenckfeld's *Passional* has appeared in at least nine separate editions. Four of these were published before his death in 1561. These were printed in Nuremberg, the main German city where prayer books and devotional literature were published during that time. The five other editions were printed in 1575, 1580, 1594, 1601, and 1705. These other editions show the enduring appeal of the book.

Schwenckfeld's *Passional* is written in German and is found in the sixth volume of the *Corpus Schwenkfeldianorum*.[7] The work first appeared in Nürnberg, Germany. The Schwenkfelder Library and Heritage Center possesses eight copies of it. The book is 5 7/8" x 3 ¾", and it is unpaginated.

---

[7] For more regarding the *Corpus Schwenkfeldianorum* see K. Meschter, *Twentieth Century Schwenkfelders: A Narrative History* (Pennsburg, PA: Schwenkfelder Library, 1984), 37–60.

Schwenckfeld's *Passional* was first translated into English in 1961 by John Joseph Stoudt on the four hundredth anniversary of Schwenckfeld's death. While the book provides an accurate translation of Schwenckfeld's *Passional*, the translation is less accessible to the everyday reader as it has lengthy sentences and uses words and concepts that are less familiar to someone in the twenty-first century. Schwenckfeld did write lengthy sentences without including punctuation. While Stoudt did provide shorter sentences than those that Schwenckfeld wrote, these can be shortened further for readers in the twenty-first century. Moreover, some of the translation choices from 1961 have since become outdated.

What follows is a dynamic equivalent translation. In other words, it aims to convey the meaning of Schwenckfeld's German in a more understandable way. Dynamic equivalent translations are frequently used in producing English Bible translations. These are less literal translations than those that stay close to each word. Instead, this approach to translation uses words and structures that are understandable to the target audience. Grammar and vocabulary are focused on the anticipated reader rather than on the closest technical meaning of the original text. The goal is to maintain the original's intended meaning and emotional response, while also making the translated text comprehensible to a modern reader.

This translation starts with Stoudt's work, but it simplifies the translation so that the modern reader may understand it more easily. It is not designed to be a word-for-word literal agreement with the German text. Words like "Thee," "Thou," and "shall" have been removed. It is hoped that the reader will still gain an emotional connection with this aspect of Jesus's life.

Some of the remarks that Schwenckfeld has in his *Passional* as represented in the Stoudt translation are antisemitic. In the history of the Christian church, antisemtism has been among our most grievous and shameful legacies. Very few Christian communities of faith were able to escape the infection of anti-Judaism and its modern successor, antisemitism, including the Schwenkfelders.

The Schwenkfelder communion of faith is linked by name and heritage to the memory of Caspar Schwenckfeld, teacher and reformer. Honoring his name in our own, we recall his perspective on

Christianity. He encouraged each one to trust a grace sufficient to reach a person's deepest shames and also address the most tragic truths.

In the spirit of representing Caspar Schwenckfeld's thoughts while rejecting all forms of antisemitism, this translation has removed anything that might be considered antisemitic. In the interests of honesty and historical accuracy, places where the adjudged antisemitisms occur can be found in the appendix.

Unlike Stoudt's translation, this one will include Scripture references that are recognized to be present by Schwenckfeld. A footnote reference is found with the text that Schwenckfeld has employed. Other Scripture references are supplied by Elmer Ellsworth Schultz Johnson who was the editor of the *Corpus Schwenckfeldianorum* volume where Schwenckfeld's *Passional* is found (vol. 6). Those are supplied in the footnote with the abbreviation EESJ preceding it.

At times, the editor of this book also provides what appears to be a Scripture reference, and an afterword provides a devotional reflection.

Suggestions for Use

The *Passional* was designed so that a reader could read one passage from Scripture, meditate on it, and pray the associated prayer thoughtfully, with one prayer for each hour during Jesus's passion experience. If one were to follow this suggestion, one would be praying through the nighttime hours. If one wanted to conclude by midnight on Good Friday, one would then begin with the first prayer on Wednesday at noon.

Another means to use this book is to consider beginning on Thursday evening of Holy Week. Begin by reading the Scripture passage and then the accompanying prayer at dinner time. Read one passage each hour and the accompanying prayer. If the first nineteen prayers can be read on Thursday evening, it will correspond with the events of Holy Thursday. On Friday, begin with the twentieth prayer and read through prayer fifty-five during the day, reading between three to four prayers each hour. The final five prayers should be used for Good Friday evening. This will provide an intense experience of Christ's Passion.

If a reader would prefer to focus on the passion of Jesus throughout Holy Week, one could read the *Passional* in this way. Begin on Sunday of Holy Week and read ten prayers per day. This will take the reader from Palm Sunday through to Good Friday. If one would like to read the *Passional* through Holy Week but have a more intense experience for Good Friday, read eight prayers per day from Palm Sunday through Holy Thursday. Then, read twenty prayers on Good Friday. For more of an experience on Holy Thursday and Good Friday, read five prayers from Palm Sunday through Wednesday of Holy Week. Then read twenty prayers on Holy Thursday and Good Friday.

Another way that this book can be used is by reading the prayers through Lent. Read one prayer per day as a devotional. Then, as you reach Holy Week, read three per day. On Good Friday, read the final five. This means of reading will also provide a focus on the righteous suffering of Jesus Christ.

Foreword

Understanding Christ's Passion correctly is good medicine for physical and spiritual problems. In every spiritual depression and anxiety, and in all assaults of sin and the evil one, our minds should go straight to the cross of Jesus Christ. We should consider that He was the one who endured so much. We should also accept with a believing heart why and how He had to endure. Furthermore, we should try to recreate spiritually within us: the entire Passion, life, and innocent death of Christ. Let us come to see that everything that opposes us in body and in soul is already seen in the Passion of Jesus Christ.

Because of the grace given to all sinners through His bitter suffering, we find in Christ every consolation, comfort, aid, and help. On the cross, the great exchange takes place. For a sinful and corrupt nature, we will receive a wholly new and blessed life. From Christ, the Well of Salvation, we obtain true piety, forgiveness of sin, and all grace, peace, joy, and blessedness. These are all shaped by our faith.

For these purposes, the following prayers may be useful. The person who fears God and wants to be eternally blessed and desires to imitate Christ's passion is urged to pray with devoted and upright heart for true understanding and faith.

Prayers in Christ's Suffering and Passion

For us Christ became obedient unto death, even death on a cross.[8] Therefore we offer praise and thanks unto him.

Prayer

All Gracious Lord Jesus Christ![9] You fully atoned for our sins by offering and presenting yourself. As a result, you made satisfaction for our sins. We ask you based on your holy suffering, martyrdom, and death, that you protect us from the snares of the evil one and preserve and secure us in all spiritual temptations. You died, was resurrected, and now live with the God the Father and the Holy Spirit in everlasting unity. Amen.

---

[8] EESJ: Philippians 2:8.
[9] All the prayers in the Passional are addressed to Jesus Christ.

1

Jesus began to be sorrowful and troubled and said to his disciples, "My soul is very sorrowful, even to death.[10]

Prayer

Lord Jesus Christ! You are the Son of the living God! In your final hours, you did not eagerly seek sharp and bitter suffering, great pain, and tribulation for fear of death, but rather out of inexpressible love for your people. Willingly, you took our weaknesses upon yourself making them your own, so that we might be strengthened. Please give me strength that I may overcome all of my

---

[10] Matthew 26:37–38.

sorrow and pain from your sorrow and be able to patiently bear all things in you. Amen.

2

And going a little farther he fell on his face and prayed, "My Father, if it be possible, let this cup pass from me; nevertheless, not as I will, but as you will." And there appeared to him an angel from heaven, strengthening him, and being in agony he prayed more earnestly.[11]

Prayer

Lord Jesus Christ! You gladly accepted fierce pain and martyrdom because of your great love for us. You were strengthened during the pain and anguish of powerful prayer by the heavenly angel! O grant

---

[11] Luke 22:43–44.

that when I am tempted, I may come before your throne of grace with true confidence so that I may find mercy and grace when I need it most. Grant that I may fully yield my will to your will which is the holiest so that all my actions, indeed my life with all my words and thoughts may be submissive and loyal to your service. Amen.

3

And his sweat became like great drops of blood falling down upon the ground.[12]

Prayer

Lord Jesus Christ! As you took the weighty burden of our sins upon your shoulders, you let great drops of bloody sweat fall to the ground. Help me, as miserable as I am, in this aimless and weary world where we work so much, to perspire as you did. Please do not let me grow weary and lazy in good works. Let me instead gain favor in your sight as I come to the time when reward will be given in the future. Help me not to be put to shame. Amen.

---

[12] Luke 22:44.

4

And when he rose from prayer, he came to the disciples and found them sleeping for sorrow, and he said to them, "Why do you sleep? Rise and pray that you may not enter into temptation."[13]

Prayer

O Lord Jesus Christ! You are the true light which shines forever and can never be put out! You have commanded us to watch and pray that we do not enter temptation! The spirit is willing, but the flesh is weak.[14] I beg you to shake out of my soul the deep sleep, yes even the great tiredness itself, so that I may be ever on the alert for the wicked evil spirits who never sleep. I ask that I may have a prayerful heart so that I may always be awake. Help me to find you and call upon you so that by your grace I may never be overcome by them. In the face of their waywardness, help me be ever more steadfast. Amen.

---

[13] Luke 22:45–46.
[14] Matthew 26:41.

5

Then one of the twelve, who was called Judas Iscariot, went to the chief priest and said, "What will you give me if I deliver him to you?" And they paid him thirty pieces of silver.[15] While he was still speaking, Judas came, and with him a great crowd with swords and clubs, from the chief priests and the elders of the people. Now the betrayer had given them a sign, saying, "The one I will kiss is the man; seize him." And he came up to Jesus at once and said, "Hail, Master!" And he kissed him.[16]

---

[15] Matthew 26:14–15.
[16] Matthew 26:47–49.

Prayer

O Lord Jesus Christ! You were betrayed for thirty pieces of silver by one of your disciples. You cherished him most dearly and yet were delivered into the hands of your enemies. You did not even turn from the kiss which the godless Judas gave to you! Please help me to treasure you deeply within my heart. Do not let me mistake you for another, nor betray you, nor desert you. Instead, let me remain steadfastly loyal forever. May this sustain my soul. Please allow me to return love and goodness for my enemies' hate and evil. Amen.

6

Then they came up and laid hands on Jesus and seized him.[17]

Prayer

Lord Jesus Christ! You willingly let yourself be taken by those who were evil, godless, and servants of the high priests.[18] You allowed this to happen so that you might free us by your chains from our own. Those chains would have led us to eternal imprisonment by the evil one. Please connect and bind my heart and mind by the sweet bond of your love so that I may always lift up all my desires, inclinations, and energy to your praise and service. Please grant that I would never oppose your holy will. Amen.

---

[17] Matthew 26:50.
[18] The Stoudt translation has "evil godless Jews and servants of the high priests." Schwenckfeld draws attention to the Jews in reading number 9, too.

7

But Simon Peter drew his sword, and struck the slave of the high priest, and cut off his right ear. But Jesus rebuked him and said, "No more of this!" And He touched his ear and healed him.[19]

Prayer

O Lord Jesus Christ! You have endless and immeasurable quantities of goodness. During your betrayal, you were willing to heal the ear of the servant Malchus, who had raised his hand against

---

[19] Matt 26:41; Luke 22:51.

you. This serves as an example that all Christians should be ashamed to take revenge on anyone and instead should be cautious of harming the innocent in any way![20] Please remove all desire for vengeance from my heart. Replace it with Christian mildness and patience. Replace the ears of my old self before I knew you. Scandalous things have been spoken into them encouraging the old self, but those pleasures are passing away. Instead, let me hear with my new self's ears which desire to listen to your word, which listen to you, which follow you obediently in whatever serves to further Christian discipline and blessedness for ever more. Amen.

8

Then all the disciples left him and fled.[21]

---

[20] I have considerably altered the wording of this sentence so as to make it flow better and be understandable.
[21] Matthew 26:56.

Prayer

Lord Jesus Christ! In your greatest and final need, you were completely abandoned by your chosen disciples. Will you please share your grace and mercy with me, a poor servant. As you grant this grace, please receive me into your company of chosen people. Nevermore, let me abandon you or error in any way about the path of salvation so that in death, I may come to you in eternal life and remain with you, my Lord, forever. Amen.

9

The Jews seized Jesus and bound him. First they led him to Annas.[22]

Prayer

Lord Jesus Christ! You chose to be handcuffed like a criminal and brought in shame before the high priest Annas. Let me never come under the power and hands of the roaring lion. That one is prowling about looking to prey upon us. Protect me Lord, that I may not suffer because of wrongs. Instead, let me only suffer for the sake of your glory, truth, and honor. As a result, may I rejoice and be glad in the revelation of your glory. Amen.

---

[22] John 18:13.

10

They were standing and warming themselves; Peter also was with them.[23] And a maid came up to him, and said, "You also were with the Galilean." But he denied it before them all, saying, "I do not know what you mean. And he began to invoke a curse on himself and swear, "I do not know the man."[24] And

---

[23] John 18:18.
[24] Matthew 26:69–74. Schwenckfeld's *Passion* does not include Matthew 26:71–73 which includes two other denials.

the Lord turned and looked at Peter, and Peter remembered the word of the Lord. And he went out and wept.[25]

Prayer

Lord Jesus Christ! You chose to be denied three times by your disciple. Afterwards, you looked on him with compassion, then he repented and wept bitterly. Please look on me today, a poor and needy sinner, with compassionate eyes filled with your mercy. Let me then, too, mourn over my sins, and may you wash them away with penitent tears. May I never again think to deny you either by words or deeds. Amen.

11

One of the officers standing by struck Jesus with his hand, saying, "Is that how you answer the high priest?" Jesus answered him, "If I have spoken wrongly, bear witness to the wrong; but if I have spoken rightly, why do you strike me?"[26]

---

[25] Luke 22:61–62.
[26] John 18:22–23.

Prayer

Lord Jesus Christ! You patiently endured unjust blows from an unruly servant. Please give me a self-disciplined and pleasant mind to moderate my unkind passions and anger so that I may show goodness and self-control to all. Help me so that my speech may be salted with graciousness[27] in order that I might be able to give proper answers to everyone. Amen.

12

Annas then sent him bound to Caiaphas the high priest.[28]

Prayer

O Lord Jesus Christ! You chose to be led in bonds to Caiaphas the high priest! Please let me never be bound to my enemies! Loosen and break the ropes and bonds of the sinful conscience! Undo all attachments to the evil spirit so that I may live in security. May I sing with David, "You have loosed

---

[27] See Colossians 4:6
[28] John 18:24.

my bonds. To you I offer praise and thanksgiving."[29] Amen.

13

Now the chief priests and the whole council[30] were seeking false testimony against Jesus so they might put him to death, but they found none, though many false witnesses came forward.[31]

Prayer

Lord Jesus Christ! You chose to be accused of blasphemy by the high priest! I plead to you that you keep me from blasphemy of your most holy name which could be shown by my words, deeds, or evil example. May no curse, oath, or blasphemy come from my mouth. Instead, may only what is godly, useful, and beneficial come from me. Amen.

---

[29] E. Johnson notices the resemblance to Psalm 116 :16b–17. In the prayer, Schwenckfeld ascribes the Psalm to David, but it is not recorded as from David in the Bible.
[30] The ESV provides the note that the council is the Sanhedrin.
[31] Matthew 26:59–60.

14

Then the high priest tore his robes and said, "He has uttered blasphemy. What further witnesses do we need? You have now heard his blasphemy. What is your judgment?"[32]

Prayer

Lord Jesus Christ! You chose to be accused of blasphemy by the high priest! I ask you to keep me from the blasphemy of your name, the most holy

---

[32] Matthew 26:65–66.

name.³³ Prevent me from committing blasphemy either by my words, deeds, or evil example. May no curse, oath, or blasphemy pass from my mouth, but only what is godly, useful and beneficial.³⁴ Amen.

15

They answered, "He deserves death." ³⁵

Prayer

O Lord Jesus Christ! You were condemned and judged worthy of death by the unbelieving Jews of that day so that you might release us from guilt and sin! I plead to you to impart your grace to me so that I may patiently endure all false witness and defamation. May I never lie about my neighbor or condemn him.³⁶ Instead, I commend you for all

---

³³ While Schwenckfeld does not provide a clear Scriptural reference, 1 Timothy 1:20 may be in mind. Speaking blasphemous words and doing blasphemous acts is what is characteristic of the beast in Revelation 13:1–6

³⁴ While a specific Scripture is in mind, several could be: 1 Corinthians 10:23; Philippians 4:8; Colossians 4:6; James 3:1–13.

³⁵ Matthew 26:66.

³⁶ A possible reference to Exodus 20:16

judgment and vengeance.[37] Protect me also, O Lord Jesus, so at your return I may not be condemned to eternal death, but rather that I will be set, joyously and blessedly, at your right hand with all your dear saints. Amen.

16

Now the men who were holding Jesus in custody mocked him and beat him and spoke other words against him, reviling him.[38]

Prayer

O Lord Jesus Christ! You chose to bear much criticism, mocking, and slander. You endured this throughout an entire night. You patiently bore unspeakable shame for our benefit. Please do not allow all the reviling, shaming, mocking, and disgrace which people may give to me, a poor sinner,

---

[37] A possible reference to Deuteronomy 32:35; Psalm 94:1–2; Romans 12:19; 1 Thessalonians 4:6; Hebrews 10:30.
[38] Luke 22:63–65.

distress me.[39] And since you, as Lord of everything, have foreshadowed all of this, may I, as an unworthy servant, patiently follow your example. Amen.

17

Then they spat in his face.[40]

Prayer

O Lord Jesus Christ! You are the eternal radiance of divine glory. You are the image of the essence of the Father![41] You did not wish to turn away your most holy face, one on which the angels like to gaze.[42] You did not turn it away from the vile spitting from your persecutors. I plead to you, let not your image in my soul be spotted and stained by my filthy sin. Instead will you, by your grace, cleanse me and purify me so that I, after the degeneracy of the darkness of this

---

[39] While Schwenckfeld does not appeal to Paul's example, the ideas of endurance for doing what is right is found in 1 Corinthians 4:11–13.
[40] Matthew 26:67.
[41] A possible reference to Colossians 1:15–17.
[42] A possible reference to Matthew 18:10.

old life,[43] may see your bright and shining face in eternal life.[44] Amen.

18

And some began to cover his face and to strike him.[45]

Prayer

Lord Jesus Christ! Gazing at your face is the highest blessedness. Yet, you let your most holy face be covered with a cloth. We ask you to lift up the light of your face over us. Never let us be in darkness. Please take from my heart the cloak of ignorance so that more and more, I disperse the darkness of the folly of this world. Furthermore, may I become filled with the knowledge of your will in all godly wisdom and prudence, so that I always perform and bring

---

[43] This points to the old man/new man idea that is found frequently in Schwenckfeld's thinking.
[44] See Revelation 22:3–4.
[45] Mark 14:65.

you what is pleasing, dear, and acceptable to you. Amen.

19

They also blindfolded him and asked him, "Prophesy! Who is it that struck you?"[46]

Prayer

Lord Jesus Christ! You suffered for us and have given us your Passion as a model by which we may follow in your footsteps! Grant that I, following this example, may in all my suffering ever resist evil and rather willingly accept what adversity confronts me with a patient and good heart. May I never be moved to wrath in any way by slander or the abuse of the wicked. Instead, may I, in all such temptation receive from you the capacity to bear all this with your grace. Amen.

---

[46] Luke 22:64.

20

And as soon as it was morning the chief priest with the elders and scribes, and the whole council held a consultation; and they bound Jesus and led him away and delivered him to Pilate.[47]

Prayer

O Lord Jesus Christ! You are the judge of the living and the dead. You chose to be led before the judgment seat of the unhappy judge Pilate! I entreat you to help me follow your example. May I not resist any authority. According to your will, I subject myself to all authorities and choose to be obedient

---

[47] Mark 15:1.

to my elders. Let me show honor and good will to all in authority. Let me live so close to you that on the day of judgment before your solemn judgement seat I may have no fear. Instead, let me be confident at that time that I will be counted among your saints and the elect who will stand at your right hand receiving all blessing. Amen.

21

And the chief priests accused him of many things. And Pilate again asked him, "Have you any answer to make? See how many charges they bring against you." But Jesus made no further answer, so that Pilate wondered.[48]

Prayer

Lord Jesus Christ! Before Pilate, you did not answer. Your false accusers,[49] laid many serious accusations against you. By a single word, but like a lamb before shearers, you did not choose to open your mouth. You also were not insolent or obstinate. Grant that I may patiently overcome all accusations, persecution and unrighteousness of my accusers by

---

[48] Mark 15:3–5.
[49] Schwenckfeld also adds "the evil Jews."

silence and never start, say or begin anything at all in an agitated mood. Amen.

22

And Pilate asked Jesus, "Are you the King of the Jews?" Jesus answered, "My kingship is not of this world: For this I was born, and for this I have come into the world, to bear witness to the truth. Everyone who is of the truth hears my voice."[50]

Prayer

Lord Jesus Christ! You are the only prince of heaven and earth. You are King of kings and Lord of all lords. When examined by Pontius Pilate, you gave good evidence that you are truly far from the kingdom of the world. By myself, I can do nothing. So, I humbly ask you, to help me to be not of this world nor to cling to perishable things with my heart, as you are not of this world. Grant that I may pay no attention to the temporal things we see but to the eternal things we do not see.

---

[50] John 18:33, 36–37.

23

Now Pilate spoke to the high priest and the people, "I find no crime in him."[51]

Prayer

Lord Jesus Christ! You are the perfect and innocent Lamb of God! You alone are without guilt and sin. Please help me to follow you purity. Let me become holy in body and soul. Allow me to hope completely in your blessedness which you give freely and graciously share with us. Amen.

In the First Hour Which is Our Seventh

---

[51] John 18:38.

24

And when he learned that he belonged to Herod's jurisdiction, he sent him over to Herod, who was himself in Jerusalem at that time.[52]

Prayer

O Lord Jesus Christ! You are the fount of all glory and splendor. Yet, you were led shamefully back and forth in the city from one judge to another in deep disgrace. They treated you like any disgraceful murderer by the wicked ways of the executioner! Please strengthen my heart so that I may not be moved by evil slander. Enable me to be strong in my inner person and be patient. Amen.

25

When Herod saw Jesus, he was very glad, for he had long desired to see him, because he had heard about him, and he was hoping to see some sign done by him.[53]

---

[52] Luke 23:7.
[53] Luke 23:8.

Prayer

Lord Jesus Christ! Your honor fills heaven and earth. You can display them when and where you want to so that people can receive salvation. However, you do not display yourself for the satisfaction of curious eyes. I ask you to drive away all pride, glory, and the search for vain honor. Let me do nothing to gain human praise, but instead let me do all things for your glory. Let me not seek my own fame, but rather the good of all people, and what improves and save them. Amen.

26

So Herod questioned him at some length; but he made no answer.[54]

Prayer

Lord Jesus Christ! You were quested by Herod with mocking words, but you gave no answer. Grant that I may guard my lips with all care. Let me not sin with my tongue. Let no useless vain or idle word come from my lips but only what is good and agreeable to hear. Amen.

---

[54] Luke 23:9.

27

And Herod with his soldiers treated him with contempt and mocked him; then arraying him in gorgeous apparel,[55] sent him to Pilate.[56]

Prayer

Lord Jesus Christ! You are the heavenly Father's wisdom! You chose to be mocked scornfully by Herod's soldiers! Please decree that I, by your grace, would rather be mocked with you than be praised by an impure and evil world. Grant that I would choose your dishonor to be my treasure rather than achieve worldly honors. Allow me to reject worldly wisdom, which is foolishness with God, and instead come to you, the source of all wisdom.[57] Amen.

28

Now at the feast the governor was accustomed to release for the crowd any one prisoner they wanted.[58] And they had a notorious prisoner, called

---

[55] The ESV uses the words "splendid clothing."
[56] Luke 23:11.
[57] The wording sounds like 1 Cor 1:20–21, 31 and 2:6.
[58] EESJ: Matt 27:15-17.

Barabbas. So, when they were gathered, Pilate said to them, "Whom do you want me to release for you, Barabbas, or Jesus who is called Christ?"[59] But they all cried out together. "Away with this man, and release to us Barabbas!"[60]

Prayer

Lord Jesus Christ! You are the living stone who was rejected by men but chosen by God for glory and honor.[61] Grant that through faith I may become firmly rooted and grounded in your teachings. Allow me to grow rich in all gratitude, so that I may not confuse you with any creature or give up on you.[62] Amen.

---

[59] EESJ: Luke 23:18.
[60] Schwenckfeld does not include the Scripture reference here. The editor Johnson notes that it resembles much of Matthew 27:15–17 and Luke 23:18.
[61] Johnson believes that a reference to 1 Peter 2:6 is present. This sounds like 1 Peter 2:4.
[62] This seems to be influenced by Romans 1:24–25.

29

Then Pilate took Jesus and scourged him.[63]

Prayer

Lord Jesus Christ! You allowed the holy parts of your body to be wounded and scourged by hard unrelenting beatings by men. By your wounds, you can heal our wounded souls, and by your stripes, you can take away our guilt![64] Keep me free from the punishment of eternal wrath which I have justly earned. Let me accept patiently your corrective discipline when you apply it.[65] Amen.

---

[63] John 19:1.
[64] This resembles Isaiah 53:5.
[65] This resembles Hebrews 12:5–6.

30

Then the soldiers of the governor took Jesus into the governor's headquarters and they gathered the whole battalion before him. And they stripped and put a scarlet robe upon him, and weaving[66] a crown of thorns, they put it upon his head, and put a reed in his right hand. And kneeling before him they mocked him, saying, "Hail, king of the Jews!"[67]

Prayer

Lord Jesus Christ! You are the true King of Glory. Yet, you allowed a purple robe to be put upon you. You allowed them to put a reed in your hand,

---

[66] The Stoudt translating has the word "plaiting."
[67] Matthew 27:27–29.

mocking you. You allowed a crown of sharp thorns to be pressed down upon your head. Thus, you were hailed as a king but scornfully. I ask you to subdue and tame the great evil of my own heart. Strengthen my weakness so that I may not be ashamed to be mocked, reviled, and despised for the sake of your truth. Let the thorns of true penitence, pain and suffering for my sins penetrate my heart, so that I willingly become fully contrite under your cross. Let all thorns of adversity that pain my flesh, all of the anxieties and temptations be like yours. Give me the strength to bear suffering in as you did. You were able to take our thorns of guilt upon yourself so that we might be brought to the heavenly Fatherland and may be made blessed partakers of your joy. Amen.

31

And they struck his head with a reed, and spat upon him.[68]

---

[68] Schwenckfeld does not provide a biblical reference. Johnson sees a correspondence with John 19:3 and Mark 15:19.

Prayer

Lord Jesus Christ! You bore all sorts of mockery and criticisms from men, but still you left us a perfect example of the greatest patience. Please give me, a hopeless human being who is worthy of death on my own, the ability to succeed rather than be overcome by evil. May I bear all the evil that befalls me with patience and finally be saved.

32

So Jesus came out, wearing the crown of thorns, and the purple robe. Pilate said to them, "Here is the man!"[69]

Prayer

Lord Jesus Christ! You were deeply wounded by sharp rods, bound, beaten, spat upon, and bore a crown of thorns. You were sent out in a purple robe to be mocked by an insensible crowd. Such an example shames our own sinful vanity. Help me to become free from all greed and worldly vanity. Please also help me to wear true divine virtues which are glorious in your sight.

33

They cried out, "Crucify him!" Pilate said to them, "I find no crime in him." But they were urgent, demanding with loud cries that he should be crucified. And their voices prevailed.[70]

---

[69] Schwenckfeld does not provide a biblical reference. Johnson sees a correspondence with John 19:5.

[70] Schwenckfeld does not provide a biblical reference. Johnson sees a correspondence with John 19:6 and Luke 23:21, 23.

Prayer

Lord Jesus Christ! You chose to show yourself with so many virtues and traits before judge Pilate that he pronounced you innocent. Yet, you were crucified because of the heated cries of the Jews! Grant that I too may not be moved nor antagonized by the envy, scorn and ingratitude of the present world. Let me not weaken or fall from the grace of Christian living and piety out of fear. Keep me from turning away from what I know to be true and what is right and good. Amen.

34

So Pilate gave sentence that their demand should be granted. Then he handed him over to them to be crucified.[71]

Prayer

Lord Jesus Christ! You willingly chose to be condemned to death. Indeed, you were condemned to death on the cross. That was not only a sharp and bitter way to die but also the most shameful. You died for my sake and for the redemption of the whole world. By that death, you not only took our well-deserved scorn and shame, but you also brought about and gave us your divine glory! I plead to you by your cross to make my short time of sorrow and temptation light and easy to bear.[72] Strengthen me in my inner person so that I may find aid in my weakness. Help me in my weakness so that I may rejoice in you forever. Let me also rejoice in you forever so that I may come to the goal of my faith, the salvation of my soul. Amen.

---

[71] Luke 23:24; John 19:16.
[72] Johnson sees a reference to 2 Corinthians 4:6 and 1 Peter 1:9

35

So they took Jesus, and he went out, bearing his own cross, to the place called the place of a skull, which is called in Hebrew Golgotha.[73]

Prayer

Lord Jesus Christ! You willingly bore the disgraceful cross. You did so when your strength had been sapped by great tribulation and anguish. You were

---

[73] Schwenckfeld does not provide a biblical reference. Johnson sees a correspondence with John 19:16–17.

drained like the martyrs and were full of dead bones. I beg you to strengthen me to bear my cross and to follow you in a worthy manner. Also, please help me so that the perverse flesh which always clings to its lusts may not cast your sweet yoke from my neck.[74] Amen.

36

And there followed him a great multitude of the people, and of women who bewailed and lamented him. But Jesus, turning to them said, "Daughters of Jerusalem, do not weep for me, but weep for yourselves and for your children."[75]

Prayer

Lord Jesus Christ! You told the wailing women who followed you to your martyrdom to weep for themselves. I ask you, lead me in your ways so that I may daily follow with them in the footsteps of your suffering, so that I may shun all evil with my whole

---

[74] This plea for the yoke to be light sounds like Matthew 11:28–30.
[75] Schwenckfeld does not provide a biblical reference. Johnson sees a correspondence with Luke 23:27–28.

heart. Let me despise all sin for which you atoned in your innocence. May I weep most of all over my own self and my wicked flesh and may I come to know the limits of human nature. Amen.

37

And when they came to the place called the Skull, they cast lots to divide his garments.[76]

Prayer

O Lord Jesus Christ! In your crucifixion, you chose to have your clothes taken from you. You allowed yourself to be hung naked on the cross. You revealed the abject poverty in which you chose not only to be born, live and work but also to die. You paid for our excesses and made rich our spiritual poverty. I ask you to take off my ragged old man and to put on the new man, who is created like you in true righteousness and holiness.[77] Please help me take

---

[76] Schwenckfeld does not provide a biblical reference. Johnson sees a correspondence with Luke 23:33–34.

[77] Schwenckfeld wrote frequently of the old man that the Christian was and the new man that the Christian was created to be. See John 3:3; 2 Corinthians 5:17; Ephesians 4:22–24; Colossians 3:5–11. He employed old man and new man so that it

off my burdened conscience and my clinging sinfulness and let me run unhindered towards eternal life. May I follow you, my Lord Jesus, who even gave up his earthly clothes. He is our author and finisher of our faith. Amen.

38

And it was the third hour, when they crucified him.[78]

---

would resemble Jesus who is the new man who is distinct from Adam as the old man. See Romans 5:12–21.

[78] Schwenckfeld does not provide a biblical reference. Johnson sees a correspondence with Mark 15:25.

Prayer

Lord Jesus Christ! You are the only peacemaker of things in heaven and earth! You chose to be hung on a high hill midway between heaven and earth that you could draw all things unto yourself. O dear Lord I ask you that you will lift up my miserable flesh which still lives on earth and is full of unholy desires into the victory of your cross. Draw it as far as is possible beyond itself with your heavenly blessing so that I may despise everything that is carnal and opposed to you. May I not admire, nor love, nor esteem anything to be great and wise but you alone. You are the crucified one. Help me to place all my love in you so that I desire you alone. Let me look only to you, think and speak only of you, take my joy and pleasure in you alone and find consolation in you alone, my Lord Jesus Christ. Amen.

39

They have pierced his hands and feet and counted all his bones.[79]

---

[79] Schwenckfeld does not provide a biblical reference. Johnson sees a correspondence with Psalm 22:16–17.

Prayer

O Lord Jesus Christ! You were on the cross and let your hands and feet be pierced through with horrible iron nails. You let your most holy limbs be stretched apart. You bore our sins in your body! Grant, dear Lord, that my old nature may be willingly crucified with you so that this body of sin may cease to be. Henceforth may I serve sin no more. Stretch out my limbs to serve your righteousness. Guard me, Lord Jesus, that by my life I do not crucify and mock you. You are the Son of God and do not deserve to be tread underfoot by my conduct. Let me bear your death in my body so that your life becomes manifest in my flesh. Grant, O sweetest Lord Jesus, that with eager and true faith, I strain to grasp your hand that is stretched out from the cross. Grant that I may live in you and unto you alone. Let me die completely to the flesh so that I may never be separated from you in all eternity. Amen.

40

And with him they crucified two robbers, one on his right and one on his left.[80]

---

[80] Schwenckfeld does not provide a biblical reference. Johnson sees a correspondence with Mark 15:27.

Prayer

Lord Jesus Christ! You were hung between two robbers and made like the godless. You moderated and killed our deep pride with your lowly humility.[81] Grant that with my whole heart, I may love your humility and willingly follow after it. Amen.

41

And then they wrote over him in Hebrew, Greek and Latin what they accused him of: "Jesus of Nazareth, the king of the Jews."[82]

---

[81] While not stated, Isaiah 57:15 comes to mind.
For thus says the One who is high and lifted up,
   who inhabits eternity, whose name is Holy:
"I dwell in the high and holy place,
   and also with him who is of a contrite and lowly spirit,
to revive the spirit of the lowly,
   and to revive the heart of the contrite.
[82] Schwenckfeld does not provide a biblical reference. Johnson sees a correspondence with John 19:19–20.

Prayer

Lord Jesus Christ! True king of all kings and lord of all things. You allowed them to put up a sign or title in three languages on the cross as a token of victory over our enemies! I plead to you to look with grace upon us and to extend the protection of your true majesty over us. Grant that by your might, I may be kept safe against all worldly danger. Keep me also from the horrors of death and Satanic plans and aggression. May I under this sign and victory fight nobly. May I through you overcome all enemies in order that I may forever rejoice in your help and salvation. Amen.

42

And Jesus said, "Father, forgive them; for they know not what they do."[83]

Prayer

Lord Jesus Christ! You are the Redeemer who wishes to forgive all people! You were so

---

[83] Schwenckfeld does not provide a biblical reference. Johnson sees a correspondence with Luke 23:34.

compassionate to the worst of people that you prayed so deeply from your heart to God the Father to forgive those who crucified you. Graciously forgive my sins and grant that I, following your teaching and example, may also love my enemies and bless those that curse me. Help me do good to those that hate me. Also, help me to pray for those that maliciously use, envy, and persecute me. Let me overcome all evil with good. Let me be so mindful that I rejoice as an unworthy disciple of a master, as a lowly servant. Then, let me even in dishonor become like you, my head and king in order that I may have part forever in your honor and glory. Amen.

43

And the people stood by watching; but the rulers scoffed at him, wagging their heads, and saying, "Aha! You would destroy the temple and build it in three days, save yourself, and come down from the cross."[84]

---

[84] Schwenckfeld does not provide a biblical reference. Johnson sees a correspondence with Luke 23:35 and then Mark 15:29–30.

Prayer

Lord Jesus Christ! You were shamefully taunted to come down from the cross. You wanted to give us an example of the greatest steadfastness in suffering unto death. Grant that I may be lifted up in you. Allow me to cleave to you in patience and hope until I reach a blessed end. Let never Satanic self-sacrifice, human weakness or the lusts of the flesh mislead me. May no intense, depressing sadness make me fainthearted. May neither life nor death, neither things present nor to come, nor any person, ever turn me away from you. Rather may I come to despise, scorn and shun all other things but You. Will you be from me the One and Only, in comparison with whom all is vain. Yes, in you all things exist and are created. Amen.

44

One of the criminals who were hanged railed at him, saying, "Are you not the Christ? Save yourself and us!"[85]

---

[85] Luke 23:39.

Prayer

O Lord Jesus Christ! You showed and confirmed your patience by bearing scorn, mockery, and insults from everyone. Then, you endured even the words of a criminal who hung at your side. O, I implore you, help this unfortunate one[86] who lives in this miserable world[87] and has to fight against many evil things. Protect me so that no harm happens to me. Allow that no evil move me to anger or to rule over my patience. Instead, may your example of patience be enough in all the unrighteousness of this world. May your example become part of the imitation of you in my heart. Amen.

45

But the other rebuked him, saying, "Do you not fear God, since you are under the same sentence of condemnation? And we indeed justly; for we are

---

[86] Meaning the one who is praying
[87] The Stoudt translation has "vale of tears."

receiving the due reward of our deeds; but this man has done nothing wrong."[88]

Prayer

Lord Jesus Christ! You willed that your righteousness be acknowledged by a murderer who confessed your righteousness. Please increase in me the virtues of true humility and lowliness so that I may really know, examine, and judge myself. Protect me so that I do not trust in my own righteousness.[89] Instead, let me become subject to your righteousness which counts before God. Also, let me share in your holiness. Amen.

46

And he said, "Jesus, remember me when you come in your kingly power." And he said to him, "Truly, I say to you, today you will be with me in Paradise."[90]

---

[88] Schwenckfeld does not provide a biblical reference. Johnson sees a correspondence with Luke 23:40–41.
[89] Johnson sees a reference to Romans 10:3.
[90] Schwenckfeld does not provide a biblical reference. Johnson sees a correspondence with Luke 23:42–43.

Prayer

O Lord Jesus Christ! Throughout your life, you demonstrated that you are truly a Savior, a consoler, and a benefactor. Nobody who wanted help or consolation from you was rejected. In sincere trust, in your precious love and goodness, I plead and appeal to you that you not leave my soul which you have created. Instead, will you turn your eyes of mercy graciously upon me, a poor sinner? Your eyes truly did look in love upon the criminal on the cross. Receive me no less than him into your compassionate heart so that I pass joyously by your guidance from this difficult life and sadness into the cherished Fatherland of your saints. Amen.

47

But standing by the cross of Jesus were his mother, and his mother's siter, Mary the wife of Clopas, and Mary Magdalene. When Jesus saw his mother, and the disciple whom he loved standing near, he said to his mother, "Woman, behold your son!" Then he said to the disciple, "Behold, your mother!"[91]

Prayer

Lord Jesus Christ! While hanging on the cross, you spoke to your dear mother and commended her to the disciple John and the disciple to your mother. You did so that you might not let any human interest pass by as you did not leave even clothing, that is, any temporal thing behind! O Lord! I plead that you grant me strength in my great weakness that all which has to do with flesh and blood be put aside. Grant that in true humility,[92] I may be concerned about eternal blessedness. I ask that I may always cleave to and with eager joy cherish

---

[91] Schwenckfeld does not provide a biblical reference. Johnson sees a correspondence with John 19:25–27.
[92] Schwenckfeld uses the word resignation.

those things which belong to you and the Heavenly Father. This is because I owe you both body and soul as I look to you for the inheritance of eternal life. Amen.

48

And at the ninth hour Jesus cried with a loud voice, "Eloi, Eloi, lama sabach-thani?" which means, "My God, my God, why have you forsaken me?"[93]

Prayer

Lord Jesus Christ! You renounced all consoling joy for our sake. You offered prayers with strong, tearful cries to God your Father, and you were heard by the Father because of your honor.[94] Grant that in all adversity I may ever find secure refuge in you, the faithful shepherd. Let me not be so feeble and rejected that I am overcome by any temptation or broken by some trial. Instead, in due time, may I find help and comfort. May the evil spirit, the enemy

---

[93] Schwenckfeld does not provide a biblical reference. Johnson sees a correspondence with Mark 15:34.
[94] Johnson sees a reference to Hebrews 5:7.

of mankind, not tear my soul apart like a fierce lion,[95] and there be no one to save it. Amen.

49

After this, Jesus, knowing that all was now finished, said (to fulfill the Scripture), "I thirst."[96]

Prayer

Dearest Lord Jesus Christ![97] You bore inexpressibly deep thirst on the cross for the sake of our salvation and blessedness. I plead to you. Quench in me the heart and love of desires of the flesh. Ease my thirst for things that are worthless such as property and wealth and the insatiable craving for evil and sweet things that please my flesh. Instead, let me thirst for you, the sweetest drink of your Sprit. Let me not rob myself together with you, or yourself with me of the highly craved happiness of salvation. Amen.

---

[95] An echo of 1 Peter 5:8.
[96] Schwenckfeld does not provide a biblical reference. Johnson sees a correspondence with John 19:28.
[97] This is the only one of his prayers that starts with "Dearest Lord Jesus Christ!"

50

A bowl of vinegar stood there; so they put a sponge full of the vinegar on hyssop and held it to his mouth.[98]

---

[98] Schwenckfeld does not provide a biblical reference. Johnson sees a correspondence with John 19:29.

Prayer

Lord Jesus Christ! Your whole life was a cross, full of sorrow, anxiety, suffering and misery.[99] It was severed from all joy. Even on the cross, you had to drink vinegar and gall[100] to atone for our insatiable lust! I plead to you to cleanse my throat which is stained, corroded, and poisoned by lust. Let me taste your sweetness so that the things which have foolishly delighted my animal nature begin to become bitter to me. In the future, let me rather endure shameful persecution for your sake than to live on in sin's passing pleasures.[101] Make sure that no bitterness, gall, or injustice comes out of my mouth and heart.

---

[99] Schwenckfeld's viewpoint of Jesus' earthly life is likely too bleak when compared with the canonical gospels. With Schwenckfeld's special interest in the glorified Christ, however, anything would be much less. Compared to Jesus' place at the right hand of the Father, however, his comments may be better understood.

[100] Gall may be either a sour or toxic liquid. See Job 16:13; Lam 3:19.

[101] An echo of Hebrews 11:24–26.

51

When Jesus had received the vinegar, he said, "It is finished."[102]

Prayer

Lord Jesus Christ! You brought about the redemption of the human race according to the Father's will. You were the priest and the offering itself. By being both you reconciled us to God. You gave yourself graciously for our salvation and well-being. I ask you for the sake of your immeasurable goodness that you would not only work the will but also the intentions of my heart and perfect all things in me. May all things that you began in me end in you and the glory and honor of your name and also for my soul's salvation. For to you alone shall all honor in heaven and earth be given. Amen.

---

[102] Schwenckfeld does not provide a biblical reference. Johnson sees a correspondence with John 19:30.

52

Then Jesus, crying with a loud voice said, "Father, into your hands I commit my spirit!"[103]

Prayer

Lord Jesus Christ! You offered yourself as a living, spotless sacrifice to God the Father. You commended your noble soul into the Father's hands with a loud voice! I ask that you will let my body and soul truly be commended to you now and forever so that the old enemy may take nothing from me which is yours. You purchased, redeemed, and acquired me as your possession. This did not happen through perishable things like silver or gold. Instead, it took place through you most holy, precious blood, which was abundantly shed for us for forgiveness of our sins. Amen.

---

[103] Schwenckfeld does not provide a biblical reference. Johnson sees a correspondence with Matthew 27:50 and Luke 23:46.

53

When he had said this he bowed his head and gave up his spirit.[104]

Prayer

Lord Jesus Christ! Our Creator, Redeemer, and Savior! You did complain when out of inexpressible love redeemed the human race through your bitter death. You paid our death by your unmerited death in order that it might be a beginning of our life! We ask you to enliven our spirit by your most holy death so that we may be dead to sin and alive to righteousness. May we grow day by day and increase in all virtues until we become perfected human beings to the measure of your full status. O Lord Jesus! May your death be consolation to those filled with sorrow, protection for those who are afflicted, strength for those who are dejected, and security for all who share in your grace. Please allow your death convert all who have turned from you so that it may

---

[104] Schwenckfeld does not provide a biblical reference. Johnson sees a correspondence with John 19:30.

bring health to the ill and a blessed end and eternal life to all the dying. Amen.

54

And when the sixth hour had come, there was darkness over the whole land until the ninth hour.[105] and the sun's light failed; and the curtain of

---

[105] Schwenckfeld does not provide a biblical reference. Johnson sees a correspondence with Mark 15:33; Luke 23:44–45; Matthew 27:51–52. It may be better to see Matthew 27:45 followed by Matthew 27:51–52. Schwenckfeld inserts "and the

the temple was torn in two, and the earth shook, and the rocks were split, the tombs also were opened, and many bodies of the saints who had fallen asleep were raised.

Prayer

Lord Jesus Christ! At your death, the light of the sun failed, the curtain of the Temple was torn, the earth shook, rocks split apart, and the dead were raised! I plead to you earnestly that the sun of your life-giving grace may never fail me. Rather, by your inspiring and permeating light, dispel the darkness, fog and gloom of the decayed old world which is my heart! Remove all hypocrisy, which is a veil and curtain. May I honestly know myself and come to sincere repentance. O Lord! Rend my heart – yes, remove this stony, hard heart, and replace it with a

---

sun's light failed." He then omits Matthew 27:46–50, "And about the ninth hour Jesus cried out with a loud voice, saying, "Eli, Eli, lema sabachthani?" that is, "My God, my God, why have you forsaken me?" And some of the bystanders, hearing it, said, "This man is calling Elijah." And one of them at once ran and took a sponge, filled it with sour wine, and put it on a reed and gave it to him to drink. But the others said, "Wait, let us see whether Elijah will come to save him." And Jesus cried out again with a loud voice and yielded up his spirit.

soft, gentle one. On that heart, You can write your will so that this dead body may, by your death, rise up in newness of life, and finally become like you in your glorious body. Amen.

55

When the centurion and those who were with him saw that the earth quaked and what happened, he praised God and said, "Certainly this man was innocent and the Son of God!"[106]

Prayer

Lord Jesus Christ! You innocent unspotted Lamb! You left us a perfect example of all patience, revealing and making your innocence evident to all people – to the false witnesses, Judas the betrayer, Pilate the judge and his wife, one of the murderers and finally the warlike centurion. Grant that I may quit and be free from all sin and failing, all suspicion and appearance of vice, so that I may not bring any offence, suspicion, or other harm upon your people. Instead, may I be a sweet and pleasant aroma to all of God's children. May I always praise you and announce to all the world those great and wonderful blessings which you have shown to us! Amen.

---

[106] Schwenckfeld does not provide a biblical reference. Johnson sees a correspondence with Matthew 27:54; Luke 23:47. Due to Schwenckfeld's high viewpoint of Jesus Christ, it is better to capitalize Son.

56

AT VESPER TIME[107]

And all the multitudes who assembled to see the sight, when they saw what had taken place, returned home beating their breasts.[108]

---

[107] Vesper time is evening prayer. It was a regular practice of Christian worship at Caspar Schwenckfeld's time. The prayers took place when lamps were lit.

[108] Schwenckfeld does not provide a biblical reference. Johnson sees a correspondence with Luke 23:48.

Prayer

Lord Jesus Christ! Although your entire life was full of meekness, humility, and friendliness, nevertheless you allowed your death to be so earnest, might, and powerful. All those who came to see this drama, when they saw what happened, were greatly terrified, felt sorrow, and beat their breasts! O Lord my God! I ask you that I many be, not only a spectator, but an imitator of your humility and your cross. Furthermore, let me regard your elevation on the cross as inspiring and glorious. May I never stop thinking about with a downcast and repentant heart (which you do not despise)[109] the good and great value of your passion. Amen.

---

[109] Psalm 51:17.

57

But one of the soldiers pierced his side with a spear, and at once there came out blood and water.[110]

Prayer

Lord Jesus Christ! Out of your dead body flowed a most blessed fountain which gives us water for purification and blood for reviving. As a result, we are purified by the one and enlivened by the other. We are washed and purified in the baptism of Jesus

---

[110] Schwenckfeld does not provide a biblical reference. Johnson sees a correspondence with John 19:34.

Christ from our impurity. Please wound my soul by the beam of your love. O pity me, for I am completely stained, corrupted, and covered by the muck of sin. Permit me to share in the mystery of blood and water for the washing away of my sin. This flowed from your holy side. May I become clean and pure and ready to receive the new covenant.[111] Amen.

---

[111] This is likely a reference to Matthew 26:28 due to Schwenckfeld's high view of the Eucharist. The ESV reads, "for this is my blood of the covenant, which is poured out for many for the forgiveness of sins."

58

Joseph of Arimathea, a respected member of the council, who was also himself looking for the kingdom of God, went to Pilate, and asked for the body of Jesus, and Pilate gave him leave. Nicodemus also, who had a t first come to him by night, came. They took the body of Jesus, and bound it in linen cloths, with the spices, as is the burial custom of the Jews, and laid him in a tomb which had been hewn out of the rock, where no one had ever yet been laid, and he rolled a stone against the door of the tomb.[112]

Prayer

Lord Jesus Christ! After your most shameful and bitter death, you consented to be taken down from the cross by prominent men of good reputation. You were anointed with costly spices and fragrances, wrapped in clean linen and buried honorably. Let me worthily receive your holy body and blood in true faith from the heavenly throne of grace as if it

---

[112] Schwenckfeld does not provide a biblical reference. Johnson sees a correspondence with Mark 15:43–45; John 19:38–41; Luke 23:50–53. He then sees also Matthew 27:57–59.

were from the height of the cross.[113] Let it be true food and drink for my soul. Let me also be adorned with precious spices, namely, with noble virtues. Preserve them in my heart so that all of the hungers and desires of the old man may likewise be buried with you in death.[114] Also let me partake of this new food and drink. May I live forever to God and to you as a new man. Amen.

---

[113] Schwenckfeld had a high appreciation for the Eucharist. Instead of seeing the bread and wine turned into the flesh and blood of Jesus, he emphasized partaking spiritually. This emerges in his comments here.

[114] The new man is also important in Schwenckfeld's thought. He places great confidence in the new person into whom the Christian is being made. This process comes from a true heart conversion, which he called the rebirth.

59

He descended into hell.[115]

---

[115] Eph 4:9–10. There is no reference to the descent into hell in the four canonical gospels. Instead, this descent into hell is taken from the Apostles' Creed. The passage that is generally considered to be referring to this is 1 Peter 3:18–20 which reads as follows. "For Christ also suffered once for sins, the righteous for the unrighteous, that he might bring us to God, being put to death in the flesh but made alive in the spirit, in which he went and proclaimed to the spirits in prison, because they formerly did not obey, when God's patience waited in the days of Noah, while the ark was being prepared, in which a few, that is, eight persons, were brought safely through water."

Prayer

O Lord Jesus Christ! You are very God, born of the true God in eternity! After your death you did pass over into spirit, penetrating hell. You visited, stormed, and powerfully subdued Satan in his own kingdom. You led and redeemed captives from the darkness of the shadows of death! I plead to you, all merciful Lord Jesus, for the sake of your inexpressible goodness, let your Holy Spirit descend today upon us poor, lifeless, human beings. Let us with all Christian believers be released from the pangs of hell, from the dark punishment of sin, and be led into eternal, light, joy, and blessedness. Amen.

60

We know that Christ, being raised from the dead, will never die again; death no longer has dominion over him. For the death he died he died to sin, once for all, but the life he lives he lives to God.[116]

---

[116] Schwenckfeld does not provide a biblical reference. Johnson sees a correspondence with Romans 6:9–10.

Prayer

Lord Jesus Christ! You are the fountain of all goodness and the one who restores humanity! You are the eternal sun who quickens, nourishes, refreshes and makes all things glad. You have graciously brought us poor human beings out of death, out of the gruesomely dark night which our sins and transgressions have made. You have now brought us into the most desirable day of joy, the day the Lord has made. You destroyed the tyrannical horror of death. You removed it through your death and resurrection. You introduced triumphant glory. The heavens greatly rejoice in this. In great mercy, you have born us again to a living hope, to an imperishable and unstained inheritance held in heaven for all those who, in the power of God, are in faith preserved to blessedness.[117]

Even though I came from the death of sin, please grant to me that I may walk in newness of life.[118] Help me to seek what is above where you sit at God's right hand.[119] Help me, my Lord Christ, to be

---

[117] This wording sounds like 1 Peter 1:3–5.
[118] This wording sounds like Romans 6:4.
[119] Johnson sees a reference to Colossians 3:1, but it can likely be extended to Colossians 3:1–4.

concerned about heavenly things and not about the earthly so that I may be revealed with you in glory at the final resurrection, at the last days when you our life will reveal yourself to us. You are the one who is, who was, and is to come.[120] You have received power, might, and glory. You rule with God your Father in the unity of the Holy Spirit, God in eternity.[121] Amen.

Prayer

O Heavenly Father! All people, races and tongues shall offer you praise and thanks for your enormous love. With this, you have so loved us that you gave your only begotten Son.[122] He was the Son in whom you were well-pleased. You gave him to death for all of us. You did so to reconcile our sins that through him we might live eternally. To you, be all glory, honor, triumph, kingdom and power, forever and ever.[123] Amen.

---

[120] This is an allusion to Revelation 1:8.
[121] This sounds like Revelation 5:12.
[122] This sounds like John 3:16.
[123] This is reminiscent of Revelation 4:11.

Appendices

In these appendices, Schwenckfeld's *Passional* is analyzed in relation to the broader Christian faith and in relation to his own writing. The first section analyzes the particular Scripture passages that are explicitly present and those that are implied within the *Passional*. A second appendix explores the way that Schwenckfeld presents Jesus Christ.

The *Passional* is then evaluated in relationship to the Lord's Prayer which is so pivotal in his view of spirituality. Schwenckfeld's attitude to prayer is then expressed by several of his other recorded prayers for preparation, confession, and thanksgiving. One appendix will explore aspects of antisemitism in his *Passional*.

The following section contains the Apostles' Creed, the Nicene Creed, and the Chalcedonian Statement. A final devotional reflection by the editor concludes the book.

The Scripture Texts Employed for Meditation in Schwenckfeld's Passional

The majority of the passages that Caspar Schwenckfeld employs in his *Passional* are references to the canonical gospels – Matthew, Mark, Luke, and John. Nearly all the texts that are used for meditation are taken from these passages. Towards the end of his *Passional,* he employs several passages from the Pauline Epistles.

The predominant Gospel that Schwenckfeld recognizes throughout his study is the Gospel of Matthew. He specifically refers to the Passion sections from this Gospel 16 times. He identifies the Gospel of Luke 14 times. He points specifically to the Gospel of Mark on 3 occasions. He then identifies the Gospel of John 8 times. Schwenckfeld has chosen to follow the Synoptic Gospels.[124] He has not chosen to follow one account exclusively. He draws upon what he believes were the most

---

[124] These are Matthew, Mark, and Luke. They are so designated due to the similar ways that they present the life of Jesus. John is less chronological in order with more teaching from Jesus in the account.

significant events found within the records of Jesus' suffering and death.

Johnson sees several references that Schwenckfeld does not state explicitly. These include references to the Gospels, Psalms, 1 Peter, and Revelation. In addition, the author of this publication sees Scriptural language to Deuteronomy, Isaiah, 1 Corinthians, Hebrews, and 1 Peter. These may not be explicit references, but the language and ideas are very similar. These are all annotated throughout the *Passional*.

In several places, Schwenckfeld blends references from the Synoptic Gospels together. This is not surprising. Gospel scholars find overlaps between differing portions of the Gospels.[125] At times, sections from one or another help to explain the other or draw out the intensity of what is taking place.

---

[125] See especially K. Aland, ed. *Synopsis of the Four Gospels* (Stuttgart: Deutsche Bibelgesellschaft, 2006). At times these stories are even in order with each other but in different Gospels. See further R. H. Stein, *Studying the Synoptic Gospels: Origin and Interpretation.* 2nd ed. Grand Rapids: Baker Academic, 2001), 35–36.

The *Passional* does not contain a reference from another Gospel outside of Matthew, Mark, Luke, and John. It is doubtful that Schwenckfeld was exposed to other noncanonical gospels such as the *Gospel of Thomas, Infancy Gospel of Thomas, Gospel of Mary, Gospel of Truth, Gospel of Judas,* etc. While some have a fascination in these gospels, Schwenckfeld did not. It is likely that he did not know them. Even if he did, he would not have included references to these. Furthermore, nearly all of them do not have sections that speak of Jesus' passion. Many of the Gnostic Gospels would have been recognized to be outside of Christian teaching. Furthermore, they are dated much later than the canonical gospels. Even the *Gospel of Peter*, which does consider Jesus' crucifixion, would have been known to be of much lesser caliber than Matthew, Mark, Luke, and John. It was written much later, was considered to be a forgery, and was known to promote the Docetic heresy (the belief that Jesus did not have human flesh).[126]

---

[126] See further H. H. D. Williams III, *Jesus Tried and True: Why the Four Canonical Gospels Present the Best Picture of Jesus* (Eugene, OR: Wipf and Stock, 2014).

The Presentation of Jesus Christ

One of the most important aspects of Caspar Schwenckfeld's thought is his view of the person of Jesus Christ. He taught with his fellow Reformers that Jesus Christ was both true God and true man. These were in unity with each other.[127] When he wishes to communicate matters of great importance, such as in his Theology for God fearing Laity which he wrote within a year of his death, he takes the largest part of this catechism to write about the person of Jesus Christ.[128]

He should be seen to agree with the other major Reformers on much of his understanding about Jesus Christ. Martin Luther insisted on Jesus Christ as having two natures – divine and human.[129] Fellow Reformer John Calvin devoted a large section of his *Institutes of the Christian Religion*, one of the most influential books in all Christian theology, to the person of Jesus Christ. His

---

[127] P. G. Eberlein, *Ketzer oder Heliger: der schlesische Reformator und seine Botschaft.* Studien zur Schlesischen und Oberlausitzer Kirchengeschichte 6 (Würtemberg: Franz, 1998), 176–77.
[128] See further H. H. D. Williams III, *Eight Writings on Christian Beliefs* (Hamilton, ON: Pandora Press, 2006), 32–116.
[129] Martin Luther, *WA* 6.511.34–39.

viewpoint of Jesus Christ affirms the two natures of the person of Christ and Chalcedonian orthodoxy.

In his *Passional*, Caspar Schwenckfeld presents the Passion of Jesus Christ in an emotive and practical way. Christians will be able to see how each Scripture text leads to an emotive response by prayer. Furthermore, each prayer encourages the Christian to become greater committed to the example that Jesus provides and that reflects his great sacrifice.

The presentation of Jesus Christ is inescapable throughout this Passion reflection. Several points, however, are worthy of notice. One thing that the reader will grasp is that almost every prayer is addressed to Jesus Christ. Within the Christian faith, prayers are to be offered in Jesus' name, which usually concludes a prayer. This is to follow several places in the Bible where Jesus asks for prayers in his name. For example, John 14:13–14 says, "Whatever you ask in my name, this I will do, that the Father may be glorified in the Son. If you ask me anything in my name, I will do it." (cf. John 16:23, 26; Ephesians 2:18; 1 John 5:14–15).

Why does Caspar Schwenckfeld address his prayer to the Lord Jesus Christ instead of merely praying in his name? This can likely be traced to the high view of Christ that Caspar Schwenckfeld had as well as the intensity that he displays for Jesus' involvement in the Passion.

Regarding his high viewpoint of Jesus, Schwenckfeld viewed Jesus as being the pre-existent Word of God as others from the broader church. He affirmed passages from the Gospel of John that affirmed these truths such as John 1:1–5. "In the beginning was the Word, and the Word was with God, and the Word was God. He was in the beginning with God. All things were made through him, and without him was not anything made that was made. In him was life, and the life was the light of men. The light shines in the darkness, and the darkness has not overcome it."

He affirms the words of the Apostles' Creed. In other words, he affirmed Jesus Christ as being the following. He was God's only Son, our Lord. He was conceived by the Holy Spirit and born of the virgin Mary. He suffered under Pontius Pilate, was crucified, died, and was buried. He descended to hell. The third day he rose again from the dead. He ascended to heaven and is seated at the right hand of God the Father almighty. From there he will come to judge the living and the dead.[130] He supported the ancient councils of the Church, too.[131]

For Schwenckfeld, Jesus Christ was the key person for salvation. One cannot help to see the intense attention that Schwenckfeld had to Jesus. Each of his prayers begins with "Lord Jesus Christ!" or "O Lord Jesus Christ!" Jesus is not mentioned in any of the prayers without the word "Lord" being associated with him. Furthermore, the word "Christ" is also connected to Jesus, exhibiting that for Schwenckfeld, Jesus is the Messiah. No consideration is found throughout the *Passional* that Jesus is only a man.

---

[130] See further, D. W. McKinley, "A Summary of Caspar Schwenckfeld's Faith and Confession of the Lord Jesus Christ" in *Eight Writings on Christian Beliefs*, edited by H. H. D. Williams III (Hamilton, ON: Pandora Press, 2006), 132–33.

[131] See further H. H. D. Williams III, "Confession of the Beliefs of Caspar Schwenckfeld," in *Eight Writings on Christian Beliefs*, edited by H. H. D. Williams III (Hamilton, ON: Pandora Press, 2006), 134-35.

With this intense affection for Jesus, it is not surprising that his *Passional* conclude with prayers of commitment to him. This can be found in prayer number sixty and the concluding prayer.

Schwenckfeld has had an interest in the glorified nature of Jesus Christ.[132] This, has unfortunately, led to some of his thinking being Eutychian.[133] This perspective believes that Jesus Christ has one nature and his humanity subsumed by his divinity. This perspective has been called "Real Monophysitism."

---

[132] See further E. McLaughlin, "Spiritualism: Schwenckfeld and Franck and Their Early Modern Resonances" in *A Companion to Anabaptism and Spiritualism, 1521–1700*, edited by J. Roth and J. Stayer (Leiden: Brill, 2007), 131; P. G. Eberlein, *Ketzer oder Heiliger: Caspar von Schwenckfeld. Der schlesische Reformator und seine Botschaft*, Studien zur Schlesischen und Oberlausitzer Kirchengeschichte 6 (Württemberg: Ernst Franz, 1998), 177.

[133] Luther believed this regarding Schwenckfeld. See M. Luther, "Disputation on the Divinity and Humanity of Christ" in *Luther's Works: Disputations*, edited by J. Pelikan and H. Lehmann, vol. 73 (St. Louis: Concordia, 2020), 263. This was presented in the Lutheran Book of Concord 1580. See the modern version: R. Kolb and T. J. Wengert, eds. *The Book of Concord: The Confessions of the Evangelical Lutheran Church* (Minneapolis: Augsburg Fortress Press, 2000). See section 262.

Such a perspective has been dismissed at the Council of Chalcedon (AD 451).[134]

Schwenckfeld seems to be confused on this matter. Throughout his writings, he affirms these ancient councils, but then he advocates for Eutychianism in places. The Schwenkfelder denomination has not held to this belief of Schwenckfeld's for decades. Rather, the Schwenkfelder Conference of Churches adheres to the Nicene Creed, Apostles' Creed, and the Chalcedonian Statement. It does value Schwenckfeld's intense interest in the person of Christ and also a heartfelt understanding of his Passion as is represented in this publication.

Correspondence with the Lord's Prayer

The Lord's Prayer was an important part of the theology of Schwenckfeld and the Schwenkfelders. As Schwenckfeld communicates his *Theology for Godfearing Laity*, he concludes this treatise with a brief explanation of it. He emphasizes the

---

[134] See further about Schwenckfeld and Christological controversies in P. L. Maier, *Caspar Schwenckfeld on the Person and Work of Christ* (Assen: Van Gorcum, 1959).

importance of praying this prayer from the heart in the power of the Spirit.[135]

While Schwenckfeld's *Passional* does not contain the Lord's Prayer in full written form, the following correspondences can be seen to it.

- Our Father – see prayers 48 and 60
- Hallowed be Your Name – Prayer 13, 14, 51
- Thy Kingdom come, Thy Will be done on earth as it is in heaven – Prayer 2, 18, 20, 54, 60
- Give us this day our daily bread – None, but perhaps 58
- Forgive us our debts as we forgive our debtors – Prayer 42, 52
- Lead us not into temptation – Introduction, 4, 19, 30, 34 48
- Deliver us from Evil (the Evil One) – Forward, Prayer 6, 9, 12, 14, 19, 24, 27, 30, 31, 36, 41, 43, 44, 48, 49, 59

---

[135] See further F. A. Grater, C. A. Williams, J. G. Gebbie and H. H. D. Williams III, "A German Theology for God-fearing Laity from Christ and the Christian Teaching of Godliness," in *Eight Writings on Christian Beliefs*, edited by H. H. D. Williams III (Hamilton, ON: Pandora Press),112–16.

From these overlaps with the Lord's Prayer, several conclusions can be drawn. As Schwenckfeld studied and meditated upon the Passion of Christ and appropriate prayer responses, much of it agreed with the Lord's Prayer. While the Passion evokes many emotions and responses, he sees the importance of the Father's name being honored and his will being accomplished. Even though Jesus is experiencing so much unrighteous abuse, he represents the virtue of forgiveness and asks those who are reflecting on the events to have forgiveness be a part of their prayer. The warnings about temptation are found within multiple places in Schwenckfeld's *Passional*. These are a warning for the follower of Jesus.

The largest number of parallels to the Lord's Prayer can be seen in the request, "Deliver us from Evil" or as many versions have "Deliver us from the Evil One."[136] This illustrates that in Schwenckfeld's mind what is taking place at the Passion was evil and not bad luck or a series of unfortunate events. His

---

[136] These include the NKJV, NIV, NLT, NAB, NRSV. While the RSV and ESV have "evil," many renditions of these versions have a footnote stating that "Evil One" may be implied.

prayers ask for protection for Christians as they consider the evil of this event.

Schwenckfeld on Prayer, Confession, and Thanksgiving

Schwenckfeld's Passional and Prayer book contains approximately twenty other prayers. These include prayers for leaders, the home, and the church. These are not represented within this publication as the focus is on the Passional. These three pieces, however, express in Schwenckfeld's own words, his intense focus on prayer. The first two are translated by Nick Pence, employing artificial intelligence.

Instruction on How to Pray Properly

> Prayer is both lifting our minds to God and having a precious conversation with our gracious Heavenly King, Jesus Christ. To pray rightly, we must set aside distractions, focus our hearts on God, and let nothing else

get in the way is truly present with all who call on Him.

Prayer should be done with diligence every day. We must cast out wandering thoughts and turn our hearts solely to Christ and, through Him, to God. We should quiet our spirits and listen for the Holy Spirit as He speaks and pours the living Word of God into our hearts.

God's mercy grants us strength through believing prayer in Christ. It protects us from temptation, helps us overcome sin, and fills our hearts with joy and peace. Through grace, we grow daily in righteousness, blessedness, and truth, remaining steadfast through faith in Christ.

Lord Jesus Christ, teach us to pray with true faith! Help us enter the spirit of prayer so we may experience what believing prayer can accomplish with You. Amen.

To Him be praise, honor, and glory forever. Amen.

Preparation for Prayer

Merciful God, I—a poor sinner—come before You and desire to pray and worship You. But my soul is so entangled and deeply stuck in the mire of this world, and my heart is so stained by sinful desires that I am ashamed to stand before Your holy presence. God, Father, eternal Good, come to my aid! Cleanse and prepare me this hour through the shed blood of Your Son, Christ. Fill me with the power of Your grace so that I may become worthy to pray.

Renew my inner heart. Remove all strange and impure thoughts from my mind and understanding. Grant me Your Holy Spirit—the spirit of grace and prayer—so that I may lift my soul out of the sinful mire of the flesh and be drawn to a true spiritual hunger for Your love, goodness, and faithfulness in all divine things.

Let me turn from my darkness into Your light, and rise from the world into heaven, from death into eternal life, seeking my salvation in You alone.

How I long to begin to pray! O God, to You I lift up my eyes, heart, and soul, and all that is within me shall praise Your holy name. Amen.

Confession of Sin

Schwenckfeld encourages the following before prayer. Now, consider your sins: self-seeking, laziness, ungratefulness, unfaithfulness, pride, greed, lust, anger, envy, gluttony, or whatever else burdens your conscience. This can include the whole evil nature of the flesh. Pray for grace and hope in the Lord's goodness and mercy. —Ed.

> Give me grace, O God, Father, for the purpose of your mercy which you promise and show to all who are in Christ! Is not this your Son, my Lord Jesus, the innocent one whom you delivered to death? As a result, I as your guilty servant can be free, comforted, and redeemed. Is this not our throne of grace? Yes, he is our only comfort and consolation in heaven and on earth. Without him, can anyone be saved? Is he not the giver,

prince and author of eternal life? Was he not renounced for a time and sank into death? Did this not happen so that he might remove our well-deserved death and for it give us eternal life?

You are the God of all goodness. You are the gentle fountain of all blessing. Consider that this our Lord in whom we believe, whom we honor and worship, is He whom you did beget before all time out of your fatherly heart as your coequal, omnipotent Son. Nevertheless, you allowed him in the fulness of time to take on and to share our weakness so that we through him might receive your divine power, strength, salvation, and blessedness. Behold your dear Son, even your divine and eternal word which came from your fatherly heart. He allowed himself to be hung on the cross in his adopted human nature for my benefit. He let his body be pierced and wounded. His hands and his feet were fastened with nails. Thus, he hung there and was mocked and condemned with criminals. He was called a wicked man by nearly everyone and was regarded as a criminal!

O my God! Let all of this remind me today of your great patience, love, and humility. Forgive what my guilty heart, hands, eyes, feet, mouth, and entire body have committed. Forgive me, Lord! Forgive me when I served sin. Forgive me when I paid attention to the evil spirit and resisted your righteousness.

O Father of all mercy, behold the wounds in the side of Christ and my Lord! Let my sinful side and all the organs of my wounded heart be healed by the healing blood which gently flowed and was poured out for the forgiveness of all my sins. Amen.

Thanksgiving in Christ

O Jesus Christ! You are the eternally begotten Son of God! You are our Lord, our God, and our Savior! We poor earthworms regard ourselves entirely worthy of you. We do not deserve your intervention. From the bottom of our hearts, we thank you for all of your gifts. We thank you for your love and faithfulness. We are grateful for your teaching and instruction. We ask you, as much as we are able, that you do not turn your reassuring face from us, even in all of our tribulation and suffering. We beg you to perfect in us the work of your love which was begun in us to your praise. Forbid the evil one to destroy the building of your church so that he might become worthless, weak, and faint in all of his works. O Lord Jesus Christ! Let your kingdom come. Assure our hearts by your truth! Seal us with the pledge of your spirit for our redemption and salvation. Pour yourself out with peace and joy in our souls.

O my God! Increase our faith and strengthen the hesitancy of our weak flesh. Let us be horrified at the wicked Satan. He is your enemy and ours. May we vigorously resist him in your truth and with your help. Help us oppose him in all of his attacks. Help us constantly to praise your glory, honor, and majesty. Let us speak and be silent, do and leave undone, as you want and as you are pleased. Please receive us this day who give ourselves entirely to you, and through you offer ourselves in body and soul and with all that we have unto you heavenly Father!

O Lord God! We ask you, let all who are of one true faith, love, and hope, indeed, let all who seek you who desire you, and who commit themselves in the prayer of believers be commended to you. Be faithful to them and to us in all tribulations and temptation for the sake of your holy name. Indeed, you are called mercy, faithfulness, love, and kindness. Grant us all an upright and godly life!

Take away all evil will from our hearts so that, inwardly and outwardly, we may so live and work that it may praiseworthy to you and helpful to our neighbor and blessed for us. Amen!

O Lord! Keep us by your mighty strength. Let us not desert recognized truth, but grant that we grow and increase in it to your glory and our salvation. Amen.

Addressing Antisemitic Elements[137]

Several places within the *Passional*, Schwenckfeld makes statements that would be considered antisemitic by today's standards. Many of the Reformers made these statements, unfortunately, which may have contributed to later German antisemitic thinking.

Although later than Schwenckfeld's *Passional*, Martin Luther wrote a short treatise about the Jewish people. His attitude may have unfortunately influenced Schwenckfeld. Initially, Luther seemed sympathetic toward the Jews but later he turned against them. This treatise, *von den Juden und ihren Lügen* (On the Jews and their Lies) was printed in 1543. Many of his statements were quite harsh. He advocates for the confiscation of Jewish literature, the burning down of synagogues, refusing to let Jews enter Christian homes, to forbid rabbis from

---

[137] The Schwenkfelder Ministerium is to be thanked for the discussion to address antisemitism. The discussion took place on October 1, 2024.

preaching, for taking gold and silver from Jews, and forcing them to do manual labor.

Schwenckfeld's *Passional* does not contain any statements such as found in this book by Luther. His book, however, does go further than what is found in the New Testament. The following instances are listed below. These antisemtic ideas were omitted in the *Passional* translation above:

> 6
>
> Then they came up and laid hands on Jesus and seized him.[138]
>
> **Prayer**
>
> Lord Jesus Christ! You willingly let yourself be taken by those who were evil, godless, and servants of the high priests.[139] You allowed this to happen so that you might free us by your chains from our own. Those chains would have led us to eternal imprisonment by the evil one. Please connect and bind my heart and mind by sweet bond of your love so that I may always lift up all my desires, inclinations, and energy to your praise and service.

---

[138] Matthew 26:50
[139] The Stoudt translation has "evil godless Jews and servants of the high priests." Schwenckfeld draws attention to the Jews in reading number 9, too.

Please grant that I would never oppose your holy will. Amen.

9

The Jews seized Jesus and bound him. First they led him to Annas.[140]

Prayer

Lord Jesus Christ! You chose to be handcuffed like a criminal and brought in shame before the high priest Annas. Let me never come under the power and hands of the roaring lion.[141] That one is prowling about looking to prey upon us. Protect me Lord, that I may not suffer because of wrongs. Instead, let me only suffer for the sake of your glory, truth and

---

[140] This is a modification of John 18:12–13 which reads,
¹² So the *Roman* cohort, the commander, and the officers of the Jews arrested Jesus and bound Him, ¹³ and brought Him to Annas first; for he was the father-in-law of Caiaphas, who was high priest that year. Schwenckfeld focuses on the Jews whereas the Roman cohort is connected with the Jews in the Gospel of John.
Annas was deposed from his position as high priest by the Romans and replaced by his son-in-law, Caiaphas. The Jews would not have recognized Caiaphas as the legitimate priest. Instead, that position still belonged to Annas in their minds.
[141] This is likely an allusion to 1 Peter 5:8 which reads, "Be sober-minded; be watchful. Your adversary the devil prowls around like a roaring lion, seeking someone to devour."

honor. As a result, may I rejoice and be glad in the revelation of your glory. Amen.

15

They answered, "He deserves death." [142]

Prayer

O Lord Jesus Christ! You were condemned and judged worthy of death by the unbelieving Jews of that day so that you might release us from guilt and sin! I plead to you to impart your grace to me so that I may patiently endure all false witness and defamation. May I never lie about my neighbor or condemn him.[143] Instead, I commend unto you all judgment and vengeance.[144] Protect me also, O Lord Jesus, so at your return I may not be condemned to eternal death, but rather that I will be set joyously and blessedly, at your right hand with all your dear saints. Amen.

17

Then they spat in his face.[145]

---

[142] Matthew 26:66b.
[143] A possible reference to Exodus 20:16.
[144] A possible reference to Deuteronomy 32:35; Psalm 94:1–2; Romans 12:19; 1 Thessalonians 4:6; Hebrews 10:30.
[145] Matthew 26:67.

Prayer

O Lord Jesus Christ! You are the eternal radiance of divine glory. You are the image of the essence of the Father![146] You did not wish to turn away your most holy face, one on which the angels like to gaze).[147] You did not turn it away form the vile spitting of your persecutors.[148] I plead to you, let not your image in my soul be spotted and stained by my filthy sin. Instead will you, by your grace, cleanse me and purify me so that I after the degeneracy of the darkness of this old life,[149] may ever see your bright and shining face in eternal life.[150] Amen.

21

And the chief priests accused him of many things. And Pilate again asked him, "Have you any answer to make? See how many charges they bring against you." But Jesus made no further answer, so that Pilate wondered.[151]

---

[146] A possible reference to Colossians 1:15–17.
[147] A possible reference to Matthew 18:10.
[148] This was changed from "the vile expectorations of the Jews."
[149] This points to the old man/new man idea that is frequently in Schwenckfeld's thinking.
[150] See Revelation 22:3–4.
[151] Possibly Mark 15:3–5.

Prayer

Lord Jesus Christ! Before Pilate, you did not answer. Your false accusers,[152] laid many serious accusations against you. By a single word, but like a lamb before shearers, you did not choose to open your mouth. You also were not insolent of obstinate. Grant that I may patiently overcome all accusations, persecution and unrighteousness of my accusers by silence and never start, say or begin anything at all in an agitated mood. Amen.

33

They cried out, "Crucify him!" Pilate said to them, "I find no crime in him." But they were urgent, demanding with loud cries that he should be crucified. And their voices prevailed.[153]

Prayer

Lord Jesus Christ! You chose to show yourself with so many virtues and traits before judge Pilate that he pronounced you innocent. Yet, you were crucified because of the heated cries of the Jews! Grant that I too may not be moved nor antagonized by the envy, scorn and ingratitude of the present world. Let me not weaken or fall from the grace of Christian living and piety out of fear. Keep me from turning away

---

[152] Schwenckfeld has "the evil Jews."
[153] A modification of Luke 23:21–23; John 19:6.

from what I know to be true and what is right and good. Amen.

43

And the people stood by watching; but the rulers scoffed at him, wagging their heads, and saying, "Aha! You would destroy the temple and build it in three days, save yourself, and come down from the cross."[154]

Prayer

Lord Jesus Christ! You were shamefully taunted to come down from the cross.[155] You wanted to give us an example of the greatest steadfastness in suffering unto death. Grant that I may be lifted up in you. Allow me to cleave to you in patience and hope until I reach a blessed end. Let never Satanic self-sacrifice, human weakness or the lusts of the flesh mislead me. May no intense, depressing sadness make me fainthearted. May neither life nor death, neither things present nor to come, nor any person, ever turn me away from you. Rather may I come to despise, scorn and shun all other things but You. Will you be from me the One and Only, in comparison with whom all is vain. Yes, in you all things exist and are created. Amen.

---

[154] Possibly from Matthew 26:61f. Other verses are likely here.
[155] Schwenckfeld states that this was done "by the Jews."

The Apostles' Creed, Nicene Creed, and the Chalcedonian Statement

Apostles' Creed

(Final Form 8th century with roots much earlier)[156]

I believe in God, the Father almighty,
    creator of heaven and earth.

I believe in Jesus Christ, his only Son, our Lord,
    who was conceived by the Holy Spirit
    and born of the virgin Mary.
    He suffered under Pontius Pilate,
    was crucified, died, and was buried;
    he descended to hell.
    The third day he rose again from the dead.
    He ascended to heaven
    and is seated at the right hand of God the
Father almighty.

---

[156] The Apostles' Creed is approximately the same as the Roman Creed from the fourth century with similar statements in the second century father Ignatius, *Letter to the Trallians* 9 and *Letter to the Smyrnaeans* 1.

From there he will come to judge the living and the dead.

I believe in the Holy Spirit,
> the holy catholic* church,
> the communion of saints,
> the forgiveness of sins,
> the resurrection of the body,
> and the life everlasting. Amen.

Nicene Creed (A. D. 381)

We believe in one God,
> the Father almighty,
> maker of heaven and earth,
> of all things visible and invisible.

And in one Lord Jesus Christ,
> the only Son of God,
> begotten from the Father before all ages,
>> God from God,
>> Light from Light,
>> true God from true God,
>
> begotten, not made;
> of the same essence as the Father.
> Through him all things were made.

For us and for our salvation
> he came down from heaven;
> he became incarnate by the Holy Spirit and the virgin Mary,
> and was made human.
> He was crucified for us under Pontius Pilate;
> he suffered and was buried.
> The third day he rose again, according to the Scriptures.
> He ascended to heaven
> and is seated at the right hand of the Father.
> He will come again with glory
> to judge the living and the dead.
> His kingdom will never end.

And we believe in the Holy Spirit,
> the Lord, the giver of life.
> He proceeds from the Father and the Son,
> and with the Father and the Son is worshiped and glorified.
> He spoke through the prophets.

We believe in one holy catholic and apostolic church.
We affirm one baptism for the forgiveness of sins.
We look forward to the resurrection of the dead,
and to life in the world to come.   Amen.

Chalcedonian Statement (A. D. 451)

We, then, following the holy Fathers, all with one consent, teach men to confess one and the same Son, our Lord Jesus Christ, the same perfect in Godhead and also perfect in manhood; truly God and truly man, of a reasonable [rational] soul and body; consubstantial [coessential] with the Father according to the Godhead, and consubstantial with us according to the Manhood; in all things like unto us, without sin; begotten before all ages of the Father according to the Godhead, and in these latter days, for us and for our salvation, born of the Virgin Mary, the Mother of God, according to the Manhood; one and the same Christ, Son, Lord, Only-begotten, to be acknowledged in two natures, *inconfusedly, unchangeably, indivisibly, inseparably;* the distinction of natures being by no means taken away by the union, but rather the property of each nature being preserved, and concurring in one Person and one Subsistence, not parted or divided into two persons, but one and the same Son, and only begotten, God the Word, the Lord Jesus Christ, as the prophets from the beginning [have declared] concerning him, and the Lord Jesus Christ himself has taught us, and the Creed of the holy Fathers has handed down to us.

Editor's Reflection

At the issuing of this book, I am struck by the uniqueness of these prayers. Frequently, western Christians bypass the events of Holy Thursday and Good Friday. For many who come to Holy Week, the attention is on the resurrection of Easter morning. This indeed is the great moment of the Christian calendar and nothing should dilute it. However, the events of Easter Sunday are greatly magnified if one has a heartfelt appreciation of what took place in Christ's passion. Thus, the horrors of Holy Thursday and Good Friday serve to make the greatness of Easter Sunday even greater.

One cannot read through Schwenckfeld's *Passional* without seeing the intense feelings that he has for the events of the passion. Each prayer with its address "Lord Jesus Christ" brings forth astonishment and revulsion at what Jesus experienced years ago. How could one not feel amazement when Schwenckfeld's prayer was, "You allowed the holy parts of your body to be wounded and scourged by hard unrelenting beatings by men" (prayer 29). Likewise, "You allowed a crown of sharp thorns to be pressed down upon your head" (prayer 30). And also, "You allowed them to put up a sign or title in three languages on the cross as a token of victory over our enemies!" (prayer 41). Schwenckfeld captures the horrors of what has happened and the tremendous self-restraint and obedience that he performed. It leads me to ask, "Have I become desensitized to the horrors of this event? Then, have I become numbed to the greatness of Christ's endurance?"

Similarly, Schwenckfeld's *Passional* is a personal challenge to obedience and devotion. This goes well beyond the following of commands, which might be shared from a pulpit or in some devotional literature. Schwenckfeld's *Passional* includes prayers for resistance to temptation, such as when he prays, "O grant that when I am tempted I may come before your throne of grace with true confidence so that I may find mercy and grace when I need it most" (prayer 3). Also, "Please allow me to return love and goodness for my enemies' hate and evil." (prayer 5). However, some of Schwenckfeld's prayers in his *Passional* extend to obedience even during times of suffering. A prayer such as "Grant that I, following Jesus' example, may in all my suffering ever resist evil and rather willingly accept what adversity confronts me with a patient and good heart (prayer 19), is an encouragement to do the right thing even when suffering. This is frequently not spoken about in western Christianity, although millions of Christians, largely from the global south and east experience this challenge as a result of persecution.

The *Passional* is in the end a correction to being desensitized to the death of Jesus, the Son of God. It is also a calling to faithful obedience. It is finally a calling to adore Jesus Christ, the Son of God, and to come to him and give him all glory, honor, triumph, kingdom and power, forever and ever.

Amen.

Bibliography

Aland, K. ed. *Synopsis of the Four Gospels*. Stuttgart: Deutsche Bibelgesellschaft, 2006.

Alardus, *Piae precationes in passionem Jesu Christi*. Amsterdam, 1532.

Bernard, *Passio Domini Jesu Christi secundum quatouor Evangelia*. Basel: Michael Furter, 1510.

Biel, Gabriel. Passionis dominice sermo historialis notabilis atque praeclarus. Germany: Heumann, 1509.

de Gerson, J. *Sermo de passione dominic: Nuper e Gallico in latium traductus*. Strassburg: Schürer, 1510.

Eberlein, P. G. *Ketzer oder Heliger: der schlesische Reformator und seine Botschaft*. Studien zur Schlesischen und Oberlausitzer Kirchengeschichte 6. Würtemberg: Franz, 1998.

Grater, F. A., C. A. Williams, J. G. Gebbie and H. H. D. Williams III, "A German Theology for God-fearing Laity from Christ and the Christian Teaching of Godliness." In *Eight Writings on Christian Beliefs*, 32–116. Edited by H. H. D. Williams III. Pandora Press: Kitchener, 2006.

Knoblouch, J. *Der text des passions. oder lidens Christi, auß den vier evangelisten zusammen inn ein son bracht mit schönen figüren*. Basel: Knoblauch, 1506.

Kolb, R. and T. J. Wengert, eds. *The Book of Concord: The Confessions of the Evangelical Lutheran Church*. Minneapolis: Augsburg Fortress Press, 2000.

Luther, M. "Disputation on the Divinity and Humanity of Christ." In *Luther's Works: Disputations*. Edited by J. Pelikan and H. Lehmann. Vol. 73. St.Louis: Concordia, 2020.

Luther, M. *Luthers Werke: Kritische Gesamtausgabe [Schriften]*. 73 vols. Weimar: H. Böhlau, 1883–2009.

Luther, M. *Sermons on the Passion of Christ: Translated from the German*. Rockland, IL: Lutheran Augustana, 1871.

Luther, M. *von den Juden und ihren Lügen*. Wittenberg, 1543.

Maier, P. L. *Caspar Schwenckfeld on the Person and Work of Christ*. Assen: Van Gorcum, 1959.

McKinley, D. "A Summary of Caspar Schwenckfeld's Faith and Confession of the Lord Jesus Christ." In *Eight Writings on Christian Beliefs*, edited by H. H. D. Williams III, 132–33. Pandora Press: Kitchener, 2006.

McLaughlin, E. "Spiritualism: Schwenckfeld and Franck and Their Early Modern Resonances." In *A Companion to Anabaptism and Spiritualism, 1521–1700*. Edited by J. Roth and J. Stayer, 119–62. Leiden: Brill, 2007.

Meschter, K. *Twentieth Century Schwenkfelders: A Narrative History*. Pennsburg, PA: Schwenkfelder Library, 1984.

Oberammergau, Germany: Passionspiele Oberammergau. https://www.passionsspiele-oberammergau.de/en/home (Accessed: 20 February 2025).

Pinder, U. *Speculum passionis Domini Nostri Ihesu Christi: cum textu quatuor Euangelistarum. &*

quamplurimorum doctorum vberrimis desup glosis: cum figuris... & cum mirum immodum contemplationibus & orationibus deuotis: non minus & de duodecim admirandis fructibus ligni vite: & stupendis mysteriis sanctissime crucis. Nurenbergen 1507.

Stein, R. H. *Studying the Synoptic Gospels: Origin and Interpretation.* 2nd ed. Grand Rapids: Baker Academic, 2001.

Schultz, S. *Caspar Schwenckfeld von Ossig.* Board of Publication of the Schwenkfelder Church: Norristown, 1946.

Schwenckfeld, Caspar. "Translation of Letter to a friend who is on the point of losing his faith." In *Corpus Schwenckfeldianorum* 1. Edited by C. D. Hartranft, 64–66. Board of Publication of the Schwenkfelder Church: Leipzig/Breitkopf & Härtel, 1907.

Schwenckfeld, Caspar. *Corpus Schwenkfeldianorum.* 18 vols. Edited by C. D. Hartranft, E. E. Johnson, S. G. Schultz. Leipzig: Schwenkfelder Library, 1923.

Schwenckfeld, Caspar. *Deutsch Passional.* Board of Publication of the Schwenkfelder Church: Leipzig/Breitkopf & Härtel, 1922.

Schwenckfeld, Caspar. *Passional and Prayer.* Translated by J. J. Stoudt. Pennsburg: Schwenkfelder Library, 1961.

Williams III, H. H. D. "Confession of the Beliefs of Caspar Schwenckfeld." In *Eight Writings on Christian Beliefs.* Edited by H. H. D. Williams III, 134–35. Hamilton, ON: Pandora Press, 2006.

Williams III, H. H. D. *Eight Writings on Christian Beliefs.* Hamilton, ON: Pandora Press, 2006.

Williams III, H. H. D. *Jesus Tried and True: Why the Four Canonical Gospels Present the Best Picture of Jesus.* Eugene, OR: Wipf and Stock, 2014.

www.ingramcontent.com/pod-product-compliance
Lightning Source LLC
Chambersburg PA
CBHW071701040426
42446CB00011B/1859